FANNY

by CALUM FINLAY

Fanny premiered at the Watermill Theatre, Newbury, on 23 May 2024.

FANNY
by CALUM FINLAY

Fanny & Creative Associate	Charlie Russell
Felix	Corey Montague-Sholay
Paul	Harry Kershaw
Lea	Kim Ismay
Wilhelm	George Howard
Clara	Jade May Lin
Director	Katie-Ann McDonough
Musical Director & Composer	Yshani Perinpanayagam
Set & Costume Designer	Sophia Pardon
Lighting Designer	David Howe
Sound Designer	Thomas André Wasley
Casting Director	HJB Casting
Fight Director	Greg Tannahill
Producer	RJG Productions
Production Manager	Toby Darvill
Stage Manager on Book	Anastasia Booth
Assistant Stage Manager	Sophy Leys Johnston
Assistant Stage Manager	Katie Crump
Costume Supervisor	Hannah Gilbert
Press Representative	ANRPR
Marketing Manager	Emma Bright & Watermill Theatre
Rehearsal & Production Photography	Pamela Raith

With thanks to Euan Jackson, Olivia Wolfenden, Chris Leask, Greg Tannahill, Jasmine Jones, Bryony Corrigan, Ashley Tucker, Lanna Joffrey, Charlotte Duffy, Lydia Fraser, Shazia Nicholls, Dave Hearn, Julie Cullen, Emily Waters, Ben Wiggins, Mariko Brown, Jeremy Lloyd, Matthew Cavendish, Paul Hunter, Hayley Carmichael, the Peggy Ramsay Foundation, StageOne, our ongoing angels and supporters, Paul Hart, Claire Murray and the entire Watermill Theatre team.

Cast

Charlie Russell | Fanny she/her

Creative Associate and co-founder at Mischief. Trained at LAMDA.

Work with Mischief includes: Katie, *Groan Ups* (West End); Sandra, *The Play That Goes Wrong* (UK tour, West End, Broadway); Sandra, *Peter Pan Goes Wrong* (Pleasance, West End, BBC1 adaptation, Broadway); Caprice, *The Comedy About A Bank Robbery* (West End); Sandra, *A Christmas Carol Goes Wrong* (BBC1); Sandra, *The Goes Wrong Show* (BBC Sitcom); Improviser, *Mischief Movie Night* (West End, UK tour); *Austentatious* and *Yes Queens*. Charlie wrote and performed a run of her first solo show, *Charlie Russell Aims To Please*, at the Edinburgh Fringe Festival in 2022.

Other acting work includes: *The Goes Wrong Show* (BBC 1); *Kat in Kite Strings* (Short Film), *Doctors* (BBC 1); *And Then There Were None* (BBC1 & Mammoth Screen); *#FindTheGirl* (BBC3 Online); and *A Twist of Dahl* (BBC Radio 4).

Charlie co-produced (as part of Mischief) the *Mischief Movie Night* London Run and UK tour and produced the new play *Piano Play* at the Edinburgh Fringe Festival 2019.

Corey Montague-Sholay | Felix he/him

Corey won Best Actor at the Offie Awards in 2023.

Theatre includes: *Bacon* (Soho Playhouse, New York/BOV/Finborough); *Dismissed* (Soho Theatre); *Wind in the Wilton's* (Wilton's Musical Hall); *The Prince* (Southwark Playhouse); *The Trumpet & the King* (Terra Nova); *Wendy & Peter Pan* (Leeds Playhouse); *She Stoops to Conquer* (Guildford Shakespeare Company); *The Whip* and *King John* (Royal Shakespeare Company); *This Island's Mine* (King's Head Theatre); *Henry V* (Shakespeare at The Tobacco Factory); *The Enchanted* (The Bunker Theatre); *Normal* (Rift Theatre at Styx); *The Hotel Cerise* (Theatre Royal Stratford East); *Little Revolution* and *ICU* (Almeida Theatre); and *Carpe Diem* (National Theatre).

Short film includes: *Kite Strings, Angry Face, Callum, Our Night* and *Home*.

TV includes: *Casualty*.

Harry Kershaw | Paul he/him

Harry is one of the original Mischief Theatre/*Play that Goes Wrong* gang and is highly skilled at improv, appearing in their improv show *Mischief Movie Night* throughout 2020/2021 and teaching improvisation at LAMDA. Harry has also appeared in a number of comedies on screen including ITV2's sketch comedy *The Emily Atack Show*, BBC Three's *Jerk* and *Cuckoo*. Harry played a leading role in *What's New Pussycat?* at Birmingham Rep to five-star rave reviews and also starred in *Good Luck, Studio*, which toured a number of venues in the UK. Harry recently finished starring as Chris in *Peter Pan Goes Wrong* on Broadway and the West End.

Kim Ismay | Lea she/her

Stage credits include: Debs in *Elf The Musical* (Dominion Theatre); Frances in *Kidnapped* (National Theatre of Scotland); Barbara in *Come Dine with Me* (MT Fest); her award-winning one woman show *About Bill* (The Other Palace); Madame Morrible in *Wicked* (Apollo Victoria, international and UK tour); Tanya in *Mamma Mia!* (Prince Edward, Prince of Wales, Novello Theatres); Lysette in *The Silver Gym*, Dotty Otley in *Noises Off*, Katisha in *The Hot Mikado* and Fiona in *How the Other Half Loves* (all Queen's Theatre, Hornchurch); Maxine in *Stepping Out* (Derby Playhouse); Baroness Bomburst in *Chitty Chitty Bang Bang* (UK tour); Miss Dinsmore/Dora Bailey in *Singin' in the Rain* (West Yorkshire Playhouse/UK tour); Flo Manero in *Saturday Night Fever* (UK tour); Miss Bonnie in *Acorn Antiques* (UK tour); May Belfort in *Lautrec* (Shaftesbury Theatre); Magenta in *The Rocky Horror Show* (Frankfurt English Theatre); *Kiss Me Kate*, *Wizard of Oz* and *Comedy of Errors* (all RSC).

Television credits include: Claudia in *Not Going Out* (BBC); *Eastenders* (BBC); Ida Hill in *The Bill* (Talkback Thames); Maxine in *Bob Martin* (Granada) and Suzie in *London's Burning* (London Weekend Television).

Film credits include: Professor in *Mamma Mia! Here We Go Again* (Universal Pictures).

George Howard | Wilhelm he/him

George made his screen debut in BAFTA nominated series, *Sherwood* (BBC One). He was a guest lead in the most recent Christmas special of *Call The Midwife* (BBC).

Stage credits include *Witness for the Prosecution* (London County Hall); *King Lear* (Bristol Old Vic); *Zombiegate* (Theatre503); *Votes for Women*, *Playhouse Creatures* (New Vic); *The Comedy of Errors* (UK tour); *The Caucasian Chalk Circle* (Greenwich Theatre).

George trained at Bristol Old Vic Theatre School, where he was awarded the Sir John Gielgud Bursary Award.

Jade May Lin | Clara she/her

Jade May Lin, originally born in Poitiers France has a French mom and Chinese dad and was raised in Beijing, China. She is fluent in French, English and proficient in Italian and Mandarin. She learned the piano at the young age of six and quickly discovered her love of singing. After obtaining her full International Baccalaureate, she moved to Italy, Florence and was trained in classical singing at the Conservatorio di Musica Luigi Cherubini earning a bachelor and master's degree in chamber music. She recently obtained her MA in Music Theatre at the Royal Central School of Speech and Drama and stared in *Follies* as Sally Durant Plummer. Jade May has had numerous recitals, concerts throughout Italy, France and China. Furthermore, she has developed her one-woman multilingual cabaret show having a passionate flair for storytelling, performance and costumes. She is delighted to be playing her first role of Clara Schumann on the British stage at the Watermill Theatre in Newbury.

Creative Team

Calum Finlay | Writer he/him

Stage credits include: *piano_play* (The Other Palace, Studio; Underbelly, Edinburgh Festival); *What Goes On In Front Of Closed Doors*, co-written with Emma Bentley, (Pleasance, Edinburgh Festival; UK tour); *Soft* (Bike Shed Theatre, Exeter).

Immersive credits include: *Paddington Lo-Commotion* (Blenheim Palace, Oxfordshire); *Peter Rabbit's Garden Adventure* (Blenheim Palace, Oxfordshire); *Percy the Park Keeper's Autumn Treasure Hunt* (Chiswick House and Gardens, London); *The Halloween Encounter*, co-written with Kieran Knowles (Luss Forest, Argyll and Bute).

As an actor, Calum has worked with the RSC, National Theatre, NT Scotland, Told By An Idiot, Almeida and Theatre Royal Bath amongst others. He is an Associate Artist of Playbox Theatre.

Katie-Ann McDonough | Director she/her

Katie-Ann is an Irish Theatre Director. She studied Drama at University College Dublin and Theatre Directing at NUIM. Katie-Ann trained at the National Theatre Studio Director's Course. She is also a trained improv facilitator.

Directing credits: *Theatrical Consequences* (Savoy Theatre); *Brilliant Jerks* (Southwark Playhouse); *Charlie Russell Aims to Please* (Mischief Theatre/Pleasance Courtyard); *A Small Family Business* (Italia Conti); *You're Alright Hun* (Short Film); *Donal the Numb* (VAULT Festival); *The Sun, the Moon and the Stars* (Yard Theatre); and *RAF 100* (Royal Airforce Museum).

Associate Directing credits: *Bleak Expectations* (Criterion Theatre) and *As You Like It* (@sohoplace). She was also the Associate Director on Mischief Theatre's *The Comedy About a Bank Robbery* and *Groan Ups* both in the West End and on tour.

Yshani Perinpanayagam | Musical Director & Composer she/her

'Perinpanayagam is a modern day musical polyglot.' Opera Now Magazine

As a multi-genre chamber musician, orchestral pianist and music director, Yshani has performed at venues from Wigmore Hall to the London Palladium, at events from Huddersfield Contemporary Music Festival to the Barbican Mime Festival, and with artists from the Philharmonia to Paul Merton. She is pianist of the Del Mar Piano Trio and Carismático Tango Band, and a regular guest broadcaster on BBC Radio 3.

Yshani was music director/conductor for triple-Oliver winner *Emilia* at the Vaudeville Theatre, *Ruination* at Royal Opera House, *Street Scene* for Opéra Bastille, *Passion* starring Ruthie Henshall, *Poppea* for English Touring Opera, *Goat* for Rambert Dance Company/Lost Dog Dance, circus troupe *Circa* at the Barbican, *Les Noces* for New Movement Collective, Longborough Opera's 2022 Waley-Cohen/Caccini programme, and with Olivier award winning show *Showstopper! The Improvised Musical*. She was Consultant MD for Olivier-winning *Wolf Witch Giant Fairy*, a collaboration between Royal Opera House and Little Bulb Theatre. She is currently music director of new music-theatre work *The F**gots and Their Friends Between Revolutions* by Philip Venables and Ted Huffman, co-commissioned by Manchester International Festival, Festival d'Aix-en-Provence, Bregenzer Festspiele and NYU Center in New York City.

Yshani's commitment to contemporary music has seen her premiere works including by Charlotte Bray, Joe Cutler, Gavin Higgins, Hannah Kendall, Benjamin Oliver, Alex Paxton and Kate Whitley. Her commissions for piano, Commodore 64 and bespoke 8-bit synthesisers have been performed at the National Theatre Riverstage, The Place Theatre and the *All Your Bass* National Videogames Arcade festival. As a composer, commissions include works for the London Sinfonietta, Onyx Brass, Orchestra of the Age of Enlightenment and St. Martin's Voices, with arrangements performed by CHROMA, Chineke! and for the Royal Philharmonic Orchestra's *Share Sound*.

Yshani was winner of the tenth Yamaha Birmingham Accompanist of the Year Award, and was a scholar at the Royal College of Music.

Yshani is one of the founding cohort of composers with Music Patron, a brand new initiative aiming to transform the way new music creation is funded by directly connecting composers with individuals who want to support them. *www.musicpatron.com*. yshani.co.uk

Sophia Pardon | Set & Costume Designer she/her

Sophia recently designed set and costumes for: *The Wizard of Oz* (Watermill Theatre); *How to Succeed in Business Without Really Trying* (Southwark Playhouse); and *Once* (Barn Theatre).

Further credits include: the UK premiere of *Head Over Heels* (Hope Mill Theatre); *Daddy Issues* (Seven Dials Theatre); *Clinton Baptiste* (Hackney Empire & UK tour); *The Moors* (Hope Theatre); *Dirty Hearts* (Old Red Lion Theatre); *A Christmas Carol* (Barn Theatre); *How to Make a Revolution* (Finborough Theatre); *Gorgon: A Horror Story* (VAULT Festival); *Faustus* (Queen Elizabeth Hall); *Neck or Nothing* (Pleasance Theatre); *The Little Prince* (Omnibus Theatre); *A Midsummer Night's Dream*, *Arthur and Merlin* (St Paul's Church, Covent Garden).

As assistant designer: *Bonnie & Clyde* for Philip Witcomb (Arts Theatre).

Screen credits include: Luti Media's *Sylvia* (as set designer); *Chronic* in Partnership with The Me Association (as production designer); and Flying Piglet Production's *Two's a Crowd* (as production designer).

Installations and site specific work includes: Glow Art's *Glow Illumination Trail* (Cobtree Manor Park), and *The Pod* (Iris Theatre, Covent Garden).

Sophia designs set and costume for numerous top UK drama schools, including Arts Educational Schools London, Italia Conti, and Mountview.

Awards include an Offie Award nomination, shortlisting for Told by an Idiot's Naomi Wilkinson Award, a year-long residency at the NDT Broadgate Design Studio and a best costume nomination at the Comedy Short Awards.

Sophia is a first class (Hons) graduate of Warwick University, and a graduate of the Wimbledon College of Arts MA (Distinction) in Theatre Design.

David Howe | Lighting Designer he/him

West End lighting designs include: *The Mind Mangler, Smoky Mountain Christmas Carol, Magic Goes Wrong, Mischief Movie Night, Mischief Movie Night In* (Streaming seasons), *A Comedy About a Bank Robbery, McQueen, Quartermaine's Terms, Bette and Joan, Birdsong, My Trip Down the Pink Carpet, Sweet Charity, Mrs Warren's Profession, Private Lives, A Christmas Carol, The Norman Conquests, The Last Five Years, Tick Tick Boom!, Maria Friedman Re-Arranged, Rent, Seven Brides for Seven Brothers, Pageant, Forbidden Broadway,* and *La Cage aux Folles.*

Opera includes productions for British Youth Opera, Philadelphia Opera, Royal Opera, and many European companies. Ballet: *The Scandal at Mayerling* (Scottish Ballet).

Broadway and Off-Broadway credits include: *The Mind Mangler, Private Lives, The Norman Conquests* trilogy and *Primo.*

UK national tours include: *Good Luck Studio, The Mind Mangler, The Dance of Death, Magic Goes Wrong, A Comedy About a Bank Robbery, Mischief Movie Night, Finding My Voice, Million Dollar Quartet, Dead Sheep, Bette and Joan, Chin Chin, 42nd Street, The Man from Stratford, Oklahoma!, Little Shop of Horrors, Singin' in the Rain, Seven Brides for Seven Brothers, Our House, Fiddler on the Roof, South Pacific,* Disney's *Beauty and the Beast, Me and My Girl* and *Carousel.*

Recent other international designs: *Sister Act, Miss Saigon, Fiddler on the Roof, Oliver* in Copenhagen, many other productions in Europe, Canada, USA, Middle East, and Asia.

Thomas André Wasley | Sound Designer he/him

Thomas grew up in Yorkshire and studied at Rose Bruford College, not in Yorkshire.

He has toured around the world with productions including: *Odyssey* (The Paper Cinema); *Macbeth* (The Paper Cinema); *Orpheus* (Little Bulb Theatre); *Touching The Void* (Hong Kong Arts Festival & Duke of Yorks Theatre); *Wolf Witch Giant Fairy* (Linbury Theatre); *Ruination* (Linbury Theatre); *GIANT* (Linbury Theatre).

RJG Productions | Producer

RJG Productions is a theatre production, general management and accountancy company.

Recent producing and/or general management credits include: *Fanny* (Watermill Theatre); *Hir* (Park Theatre); *It's Headed Straight Towards Us* (Park Theatre); *Boy Parts* (Soho Theatre); *Othello* (Riverside Studios); *Bitter Lemons* (Pleasance & Bristol Old Vic); *Polko* (Paines Plough); and *Earshot* (UK tour).

Other credits include: *Amélie the Musical* (Criterion Theatre, West End); *Brilliant Jerks* (Southwark Playhouse); *A Hundred Words for Snow* (Trafalgar Studios, UK tour & VAULT Festival); and the original production of *ANNA X* by Joseph Charlton.

Projects in development include *Attrition* by Tatty Hennessy, a commission as part of the Writers' Guild of Great Britain New Play Scheme.

The company is run by Rebecca Gwyther, a StageOne supported producer and ICAEW ACA qualified Chartered Accountant. Rebecca is also a Trustee for Get into Theatre and Mercury Musical Developments, and on the board of the League of Independent Producers.

For the Watermill Theatre

Artistic Director and Joint CEO **Paul Hart**
Executive Director and Joint CEO **Claire Murray**
Finance Director **Kim Austen**
Payroll Officer **Neil Ferris**
Theatre Administrator **Emily Beck**
Producer **Jonathan Brindley**
Associate Director **Abigail Pickard Price**
Casting and Producing Assistant **Cydney Beech**
Development Director **Steph Dewar**
Development Officer **Lucy Simpson**
Marketing Director **Emma Bright**
Marketing Officer **Robert Nesbitt**
Social Media and Marketing Assistant **Patrick Swain**
National Press and Publicity **Arabella Neville-Rolfe**
Sales and Box Office Manager **Emma Gradwell**
Box Office Co-ordinator **Carys Muirhead-Davies**
Box Office Assistants **Anita Anderson, Holly Lucas, Sam Schrijver, Mel Tucker** (full-time), **Nancy Williams**
Customer Experience Trainee **Joshua Allen**
Front of House Manager **Julie ann Jones**
Deputy Front of House Managers **Lorraine Buckle, Lesley Cain**
Head of Technical **Thom Townsend**
Theatre Technician **Ruth Corris**
Production Crew **Nick Harrison, Lawrence T Doyle, Chris Moore**
Company Stage Manager **Cat Pewsey**
Head of Wardrobe **Hannah Gilbert**
Wardrobe Department **Ros Kitson, Caroline Williams**
Operations Manager **Charley Hart**

Facilities Manager **Paul Riddlesden**

Maintenance Manager **John Ball**

Outreach Director **Heidi Bird**

Outreach Assistant **Matty Green**

Community Associates **Lixi Chivas, Angharad Arnott Phillips**

Careers in the Arts Project Lead **Angharad Warren**

Careers in the Arts Project Facilitator **Aimee Winch**

Freelance Facilitators **Lloyd Clements Hart, George Craik, Sophie Boyce Couzens, Joe Evans, Autumn Fenn, Katie Goad, Lizzie Lewis, Charlotte Moulton-Thomas, Jacky Purtill, Helen White**

Housekeeper **Karen Calder-Hoath**

Assistant Housekeepers **Beverley Bradley, Denise Dawson, Irena Dilly, Rhona Scanlon**

Catering Manager **Paul Davies**

Assistant Catering Manager **Kimberley Simmonds**

Chefs **Lee Booth, Mark Calder-Hoath, Grahame Simmonds**

Catering Administrator **Sharon Shanehchi**

Board of Trustees **Andrew McKenzie** (Chairman), **Katie Breathwick** (Deputy Chair), **Sunny Bansal, Judith Bunting, Becca Chadder, David Grindrod, Nick Humby, Rosanna Jahangard, Simon Parsonage, Danni Powell, Craig Titley-Rawson, Tom Wentworth, Maggie Whitlum, Howard Williamson**

Watermill Guardians **Carole-Ann Armstrong, Tony Ayers, Ralph Bernard, Deborah Puxley, Andrew Tuckey**

FANNY

Calum Finlay

Thanks

For FMB.

Special thanks to: Rebecca Gwyther, Susan Finlay, Katie-Ann McDonough and Charlie Russell.

Thanks to: Mark Bentley, Hayley Carmichael, Philip Carne, Matthew Cavendish, Bryony Corrigan, Kate Cresswell, Julie Cullen, Charlotte Duffy, Lydia Fraser, Paul Hart, Dave Hearn, George Howard, Paul Hunter, Kim Ismay, Lanna Joffrey, Harry Kershaw, Chris Leask, Jeremy Lloyd, Jade May Lin, Corey Montague-Sholay, Claire Murray, Yshani Perinanayagam, Jasmine Jones, Shazia Nicholls, Megan Smith, Greg Tannahill, Ashley Tucker, Emily Waters, Ben Wiggin, Playbox Theatre and The Peggy Ramsay Foundation.

Characters

FANNY MENDELSSOHN BARTHOLDY, *later Hensel*
FELIX MENDELSSOHN BARTHOLDY, *Fanny's younger brother*
PAUL MENDELSSOHN BARTHOLDY, *Fanny's youngest brother*
LEA MENDELSSOHN BARTHOLDY, *Fanny's mother*
WILHELM HENSEL, *a suitor*
CLARA SCHUMANN, *a young pianist and aspiring composer*
QUEEN VICTORIA
PRINCE ALBERT
MAN 1
MAN 2
BOATSWAIN
LANDLADY
DRIVER
STAGE BOY
STAGEHAND
MAESTRO

The play is loosely based on events that took place between 1826 and 1846.

Music

Wherever possible all onstage music should be played live by the actors.

In the original production existing recordings were used for all the non-diegetic orchestral works conducted by Fanny. All diegetic music mentioned in the script was performed live by the actors – however, this could easily be replaced by recordings with the actors miming, if required.

The sheet music for all the music mentioned in the script is available to download for free via the Petrucci Music Library (imslp.org) with the exception of music that was composed for the original production.

Setting

1. The Mendelssohn-Bartholdy family music room, Berlin
2. The same, a few minutes later, Berlin
3. The docks, Hamburg
4. A tavern near the docks, Hamburg
5. The docks, Hamburg
6. A cargo ship, the North Sea
7. Carriages, London
8. The streets, London
9. Backstage at the Royal Palace, London
10. Onstage at the Royal Palace, London
11. The Hensel family music room, Berlin

Further Reading

Endnotes are included within the script. They're intended to provide some additional biographical information about the events which inspired the play.

Additionally, the biography *Fanny Mendelssohn* by Francoise Tillard, the publication *The Letters of Fanny Hensel to Felix Mendelssohn* by Marcia Citron and the documentary *Fanny: The Other Mendelssohn* by Sheila Hayman, were key source materials for the script.

Note on the Text

A dash (–) at the end of a line indicates an interruption or unfinished thought.

This text went to press before the end of rehearsals and so may differ slightly from the play as performed.

PART ONE

Pre-set: as the audience is seated, there are the sounds of an orchestra tuning up.

Music: 'Mass in B Minor, BWV 323: Cum Sancto Spiritu (Chorus)', J. S. Bach.[1]

FANNY MENDELSSOHN BARTHOLDY *is centre-stage, wielding her baton, conducting an orchestra in her head. She waves the orchestra to an immediate silence around bar 30.*

FANNY. Just the altos. Bars 21–25.

They sing. She stops them.

More diaphragm if you can please. Again.

They sing. She stops them.

Try imagining that you've just been told a joke. No 'H' obviously. Thank you.

They sing. She shouts over them:

A funny joke! Funnier! Even funnier! Stop, stop...

She stops them.

Listen to the basses. Same bars, just the basses.

They sing – almost in the style of the Laughing Policeman. She stops them.

You see? Got that? Thank you. Let's go back to the top please, everybody.

She counts them in. She stops them in bar 3.

Tromba One, bar 1.

They play (one note).

Again.

They play it again.

Yes… you're coming off the back of the previous movement. It's conclusive, not provocative, please. Again.

They play it again.

With me, previous bar – Oom bah-diddle-um-bum-bum-bum-BAH

They play it again – a bit softer.

Lightly. Land it but lightly. Again.

They play it again – a bit slower.

Try again.

They play it again – it squeaks.

Oops. Again.

They play it again.

Better. From the top.

FANNY *counts them in. The orchestra plays.*

Tromba One plays exactly as they did before. FANNY *shakes her head. An echoey voice shouts…*

VOICE (*off*). Fanny? Fanny!

FANNY *looks around as she conducts – where's the voice coming from?*

Fanny!

The orchestra gets louder and louder. FANNY *shouts over them…*

FANNY. Who's trying to get my attention? Is it you, woodwind?

FELIX. Fanny!

SNAP! Silence. We are suddenly in the Mendelssohn family home. FELIX MENDELSSOHN BARTHOLDY, *the younger brother of* FANNY, *is seated at a grand piano.* FANNY *looks at him as if she's come out of a reverie.*

Fanny!

FANNY. What?

FELIX. You weren't listening!

FANNY. Yes I was.

FELIX. You were in your head again! Was it Wagner?

FANNY. No!

FELIX. Was it Liszt?

FANNY. No, it was Bach – because you're off to the Sing-Akademie I suppose. Though if you're late, brother, they may give the directorship to someone else.[2]

FELIX. Who?

FANNY. I don't know. Grell?

FELIX. A blockhead.[3]

FANNY. Rungenhagen.

FELIX. I will die if they give it to Rungenhagen!

FANNY. He was the former director's assistant.

FELIX. In London I overheard people saying that they think I'm better than Mozart. Mozart! Did you hear me? They said I'm better than Mozart. You say it. Say I'm better than Mozart.

FANNY. I think you're better than most are, brother.

FELIX. What?

FANNY. You're better than most are.

FELIX. I've told you the Queen of England likes my work?[4]

FANNY. Once or twice! Look, you are not the only one with important things to do today. Either play or leave me to go and tie a ribbon in my hair.

FELIX. This is for the wedding of Oberon and Titania.

> FELIX *plays a simplified version of...*

> *Music:* A Midsummer Night's Dream, *'Incidental Music, Op. 61, MWV M:13 No. 9 Wedding March'* Mendelssohn.[5]

> FANNY *stops him.*

FANNY. Stop, Felix, stop! You're making me wish I was Beethoven!

FELIX. D*eaf*?

FANNY. D*ead*! You want to be better than Mozart? Where're the inner voicings, the variations, a little modulation, even? You are brilliant, brother, but history will not remember you for having written this!

FELIX. Then fix it!

FANNY. Move over.

FELIX. Is it that bad?

FANNY. Where's the dissonance? Try the first chord in the relative minor.

FELIX. Really?

> FANNY *demonstrates – she includes the trumpet intro. As she plays:*

FELIX. Trumpets?

FANNY. Trumpets.

> *As* FANNY *plays the first chord:*

FANNY. You see? More dissonance![6] A wedding march needs to feel like it might be going somewhere.

FELIX. Yes – distract Titania from the truth.

> FELIX *begins scribbling on the manuscript – talking as he does so.*

I wish we were always together.

FANNY. On any other day I might feel the same.

FELIX. Maybe you could travel in my pocket! Then you could see what a strange and eccentric place the world really is, Fanny. And whenever I needed you, you could sit on my shoulder and wave your little magic baton over whatever it is I'm working on.

FANNY. My world is here, brother, within our home – and I happen to like it very much.

FELIX. Well. Good! As it should be! You know, I'm told some women are *swimming* now, Fanny.

FANNY. Swimming?[7]

FELIX. In the *sea*!

FANNY. Well, I'm no *femme libre*,[8] brother! Will you excuse me now, Felix? Please?

FELIX. You're obsessed with this ribbon!

FANNY. Well… Herr Hensel is coming…

FELIX. Oh God…

FANNY. What?

FELIX. You're grinning!

FANNY. That's allowed, isn't it?

FELIX. He's entirely unmusical you know!

FANNY. So? Enlightened people consider contrasts and opposites as enriching, brother. As long as he knows a French horn from a French kiss I don't care.

FELIX. I'm going to be sick.

FANNY. Will you let me go, brother, please?

FELIX. Fine.

PAUL (*off*). Fanny!

FANNY. Oh no. Felix, I promised Paul that – can you deal with him –

The door opens and PAUL MENDELSSOHN BARTHOLDY, FANNY*'s youngest brother, tries to enter with his cello.*⁹

PAUL. Ah, there you are!

Perhaps PAUL *is carrying his cello horizontally and struggles to get it through the door. Eventually, he's in...*

We need wider doors. Fanny –

FANNY. You'll have to talk to Felix. I want to tie a ribbon in my hair.

PAUL. He'll be lucky to have you – even *sans* ribbon.

FANNY. The ribbon is for me, not Herr Hensel.

FELIX. And, we're working, Paul.

PAUL. I know – and can I just say, and this goes without saying, but I am, it looks like, going to say it anyway, that the addition of an F-sharp to that first chord was inspired, Fanny.

FANNY. You were listening at the door?[10]

PAUL. Well, what else am I to do?! You won't let me join in! And, can I just say, I think, Felix, it's one of the most memorable things you've ever written.

FELIX. You see! Thank you, Paul, perhaps you do have an ear for music.

PAUL. A good ear?

FELIX. Just an ear.

FANNY. Will you both excuse me?

PAUL. Wait!

FANNY. Paul, I've other things to do today.

PAUL. Just listen! Listen to 'Paul's Theme' and give it a number, out of five.

FELIX. Again with the numbers!

PAUL. I like numbers.

FANNY. Then work in a bank![11] You cannot quantify art, Paul.

PAUL. You think I make art?

FANNY. I'm sorry, Paul, but you'll have to wait until after Herr Hensel's visit.

PAUL. But, can I just say –

FANNY. No! I will listen to you only after Herr Hensel has gone.

FANNY is about to exit. LEA MENDELSSOHN BARTHOLDY *enters.*

LEA. Get away from that piano!

FANNY is nowhere near the piano.

FANNY. I'm nowhere near –

LEA. Not today, Fanny! Not today! Come here – show me your fingers. Are you wearing pockets?!

FANNY. No.

LEA. Empty them! Paul!

PAUL *is brought over to collect things as* FANNY *removes them from her pockets.*

FANNY. I thought I looked agreeable.

LEA. Did you. Bite your lips. Harder. What do you want a pocketbook for?

FANNY. For writing things down.

LEA. Bite them harder! We read, we don't write. Felix, fetch an orange.

FANNY. Please no.

LEA. Not no – yes. Now, Felix.

FELIX *exits.*

FANNY. It stings!

LEA. That's rather the point. Right – is that everything?

FANNY. Yes.

LEA eyeballs FANNY. FANNY reluctantly pulls a conductor's baton from her pocket and gives it to PAUL.

LEA. Get rid of it all.

PAUL. Yes, Mother.

LEA. Now show me your fingers. Okay…

From behind LEA, PAUL indicates to FANNY where he's putting the baton.

Turn them over. What's that?

FANNY isn't really concentrating on her mother.

FANNY. I don't know. A thumb?

LEA. You have a blister! You're like a workman!

FANNY snatches her hands back.

FANNY. You never say anything nice to me!

LEA. You never give me cause. Why aren't you holding a handkerchief?

FANNY. Must I hold a handkerchief?

LEA. Must you? Must you? Yes! Yes, you must!

FANNY. Why?

LEA. Don't ask why! You are forever asking why! Why this, why that. You'll bore Herr Hensel half to death if you keep on at him the way you keep on at me.

PAUL. Here, you can have my handkerchief, Fanny.

LEA. No! No! You mustn't let Herr Hensel see you with another man's handkerchief! Have you not read *Othello*,[12] daughter?

FANNY. Have you?

LEA. It's all about a handkerchief, isn't it?

FELIX *enters holding an orange* – LEA *doesn't look at him*.

Ah, good – squirt it in your sister's eyes.

PAUL. Mother!

LEA. You want her to have nice dilated pupils, don't you?

FELIX *hides the orange*.

FELIX. We were out of oranges, Mother.

LEA. Oh, look! Look! I can see your petticoats! Do we have any lemons?

FELIX. No.

LEA. Arsenic?

FANNY. Don't fret, Mother – I can fix myself!

LEA. The shame of it!

FELIX *has started eating the orange*.

FANNY. What shame, Mother? It is only you and Paul and Felix.

LEA. Only me and Paul and Felix, she says! As if seeing my daughter debase herself doesn't make me want to take up the flute!

FANNY. The flute?

LEA. I shall need a new hobby if I am to cope with all the shame. What are you eating?

FELIX. Nothing.

He keeps eating.

FANNY. Paul, how do you think I look?

PAUL. Five.

LEA. Out of five?!

PAUL. Absolutely – and can I just say that I expect Herr Hensel will be compelled to sculpt you from marble!

LEA *shoots a look at* PAUL.

Or, well, maybe just paint you, with watercolours, or sketch you, lightly, with a small pencil.

LEA. Paul, leave us!

PAUL. Yes, of course.

FELIX. Yes, Paul, we're working here.

LEA. You too!

FELIX. Me?

LEA. Yes.

FELIX. But, Mother, we're working.

LEA. There's more to life than music, isn't that right, Fanny?

Before FANNY *can answer…*

PAUL. I like anchovies, for example.

LEA. Well, there you are, Paul likes anchovies. Go, boys, go, love needs space to grow.

FELIX. I think she's already in love, Mother.

LEA. Does someone else have the key to your heart?

FELIX. It has eighty-eight keys I think, mother.

LEA *doesn't look well.*

FANNY. Mother?

LEA. I feel weak.

FANNY. Is there numbness? Give me your hands.

LEA. I'm fine, I'm fine! It's just your brother, he's going to force me over the privy with his abominable wordplay – it's revolting. Get off me. Leave my hands alone.

PAUL. Can I just say, I'm funny too, Mother.

FANNY. Who told you that?

PAUL. I'm just a funny boy.

LEA. Go! Everyone go!

FELIX. Fine. Mother, if Clara comes, will you send her up?

FANNY. Frau Schumann?

FELIX. She's written something apparently.

FANNY. I've written –

LEA. Boys! Go!

> FELIX *and* PAUL *exit*.
>
> Fanny, come, sit down next to me for a moment. Imagine I'm Herr Hensel, what might you say to me?

FANNY. How did you get into the house!

LEA. I was permitted by someone very, very charming.

FANNY. Not by my mother then.

LEA. Yes, by her! And I hope that I shall quickly step into her circle.

FANNY. I wouldn't bother, sir, she's thinking about taking up the flute.

LEA. Insufferable…!

FANNY. You're supposed to say nice things to a lady, sir.

LEA. What if I start saying nice things in *Latin*? What then?

FANNY. Latin?

LEA. Yes. You might notice that I'm a little different from Herr Hensel who left five years ago.

FANNY. More than a little.

LEA. What if I have started dressing up in silly robes and smelling of incense?

FANNY. Oh, I see.

LEA. Yes – what then?

FANNY. I'm sure it is still possible to love a Catholic.[13]

LEA. Do you mean that?

FANNY. It could be our little secret, Herr Hensel?[14]

LEA. Well now you can be assured that before I get anywhere near you, I shall be talking to the charming woman who permitted me an audience.

FANNY. So definitely not my mother then?

LEA. Do you really not think your mother's charming?

FANNY. She's never said anything charming to me. But you could, couldn't you, Herr Hensel? That's something suitors do. Say something nice about me.

LEA. You've got a strong forehead and a good dowry.

FANNY. I have my mother to thank for both.

LEA. For both?! Both! That's enough! Go and tie your hair with ribbon, please.

FANNY. Sir?

LEA. Go, Fanny! Now! Tie your hair with ribbon!

FANNY. Of course, Mother – the russet one?

LEA. Chestnut! It's a chestnut ribbon. Russet is for hussies.

FANNY. Mother – you can't say that!

LEA. I can say whatever I want. And hurry Felix along, will you?

FANNY *is about to exit*.

FANNY. Mother... will he definitely be given the job?

LEA. Of course he will.

FANNY. There's revolution in Europe and Berlin doesn't seem to have budged an inch.

LEA. What do you know about Europe?

FANNY. I read the paper! Should Felix not go and carve out his place in the world? The Queen of England likes his work!

LEA. Oh, no she doesn't...

FANNY. She has said as much to him!

LEA. Well, sort of, yes, I suppose she thinks she likes his work, but, would you not rather he was here, with you, as opposed to galavanting about Europe? You're not getting much of a critical voice from me or, heaven forbid, Paul.

PAUL (*off*). Hey!

FANNY *kicks the door.*

Ow!

FANNY. As a matter of fact, Felix was suggesting that I should galavant with him.

There's a moment – LEA *stiffens*, FANNY *senses it.*

LEA. Was he?

FANNY. He was teasing me, I expect.

LEA. Yes, I expect he was.

FANNY. Besides, it would be utterly impractical.

LEA. Utterly.

FANNY. I mean, can you imagine me travelling the world, Mother?

LEA. Imagination requires hope to triumph over experience, Fanny – I haven't imagined anything for years. But I know you, you wouldn't like the world – it's too colourful, it's exaggerated and silly.

FANNY. I suppose travelling in his pocket is rather silly.

LEA. It's not real. This is real. Our world. Here.

FANNY. Yes.

LEA. And it's lovely! And Herr Hensel is coming today! It's an exciting day!

FANNY. It is. Very. Excuse me, Mother. I must tie a *chestnut* ribbon in my hair. Out of the way, Paul.

FANNY *opens the door to exit and reveals* PAUL (*who's been at the keyhole*). FANNY *exits.*

LEA (*shouting off*). Oh! And take a good look at your *father's* portrait on the way up to your room!

PAUL *comes into the room.* LEA *touches her forehead.*

It's about the only thing I haven't given her!

PAUL. You also didn't give her the truth about Queen Victoria.

LEA. Shhhh!

PAUL. What? Queen Victoria?

LEA. Shhhh!

PAUL. Why? Is it a secret?

LEA. Of course it's a secret!

PAUL. Oh, that's brilliant…! Why?

LEA. Why do you think?

PAUL. Are we to surprise her with it?

LEA. You heard her, Paul. Can you imagine if she knew the Queen of England's favourite piece of music was hers![15] And music is not her destiny, it cannot be. For her music can, and must, be only an ornament![16]

The doorbell rings.

That is her destiny ringing the bell! Fetch up Herr Hensel, please.

PAUL. Of course.

LEA. And, Paul, perhaps you could discover something of him.

PAUL. Of course – what?

LEA. Well, they say everyone who visits Rome gets swept away.

PAUL. Swept away?

LEA. Exactly.

PAUL. To sea?

LEA. By the Roman Catholic Church.

PAUL. I see. So what do you want me to do?

LEA. Well, you're perceptive, aren't you, Paul?

PAUL. Yes, very. What are you getting at?

LEA. Well you've heard that his sister has converted – she's a Catholic mystic!

PAUL. I understand.

LEA. Do you?

PAUL. No.

LEA. For goodness' sake! Find out if he's still a Lutheran!

PAUL. You mean that I should begin an intense spiritual discussion of a controversial partisan issue between here and the door?

LEA. Yes! Go, Paul, go!

PAUL *exits*. FELIX *enters*.

FELIX. Is it Clara?

LEA. It will be Herr Hensel. Go and fetch Fanny. And then you must go, Clara can wait until you're back.

FELIX. Yes, Mother.

LEA. And listen to me, Felix: be careful of planting seeds – they grow.

FELIX. I'm well aware.

LEA. Fanny wants for nothing here. She has a harmonious life.

FELIX. Until you bring in the clod honking away on a bassoon!

LEA *is furious her son has spoken to her like that*.

I can say what I want, Mother, I'm a man now.

LEA *is unwavering*.

Sorry.

LEA. It's time to fill your father's shoes. I hear them coming. Go. Go!

FELIX *exits.* LEA *grabs a book from the shelf and dashes towards a chair. She catches sight of herself in a mirror and quickly checks her forehead. The door opens and* LEA *quickly reclines on a chair.*

PAUL *enters with* WILHELM HENSEL.

PAUL. This way, Herr Hensel. Allow me to introduce Frau Mendelssohn-Bartholdy.

LEA. Herr Hensel, you've caught me reading! I was just beginning another Shakespeare.

LEA *quickly glances at the front of the book.*

LEA. '*As You –*'

WILHELM. '*Like it*'?

LEA. Not sure – too early to tell. Though five years is a long time to be away, you look well, Herr Hensel. I don't usually condone aphorisms but you may be proof that one gets better with age.

WILHELM. There's a plum in my fruit bowl that would disagree.

PAUL. Can I just say, don't eat it.

LEA. What?

PAUL. It would be a mistake to eat it. In my experience.

WILHELM. May I saying: *buongiorno*.

LEA. Latin?

WILHELM. *Italien*.

LEA. Sweet. How was the walk from the door, Paul?

PAUL. Oh, uh, unsuccessful.

WILHELM. I disagree, I've been waiting five years to get my foot in the door here, so to speak.

LEA *gets a little sweaty at the pun and steps away from* WILHELM.

LEA. I forgot you like to pun.[17]

WILHELM. Always. My theory is that only thieves dislike puns.

PAUL. Why is that?

WILHELM. Because they take things literally.

LEA. Oh God – Paul, open a window, get some air in here. Yes, well, Herr Hensel, as Goethe points out, enthusiasm of any kind is of great value so long as we are not carried away by it. So, no more jokes. You found out nothing, Paul?

PAUL. Nothing.

LEA. Useless! Do you like Gregorian chants, Herr Hensel?

WILHELM. Not particularly.

LEA. Incense?

WILHELM. No.

LEA. Big hats?

WILHELM. Hate them.

LEA. Not a Catholic, Paul!

WILHELM. If I'd enjoyed the incense you would've been incensed, yes?

LEA lets out a slightly pained noise.

LEA. Sorry. And of course, money is not important in the slightest, but you do have a better job now, yes? You paint for the King? Yes? Yes?

WILHELM. Yes.

LEA. Good, good, that's good, you've kept your word. The same can be said for Fanny – you should know that she's been developing happily and freely among exceptional company.

WILHELM. Wonderful! May I say, I'm excited to see her again. Her music stayed in my heart every minute that we were asunder. I adore it so unendingly!

LEA. You ought not to say such things.

WILHELM. I was speaking what I feel, not what I ought to say.

LEA. You're not in the lemon groves any more, Herr Hensel. It's indecorous to be so flamboyantly gooey.

WILHELM. Oh. Sorry.

PAUL. Speaking of which, and far from me to overstep, or indeed over-speak, in what is, I'm sure you'll both agree, a romantic matter, and in almost every sense nothing at all to do with me, but can I just say, I wonder if Mother ought to see what's in your hand, Herr Hensel.

WILHELM. Oh, a small poem. A token for your daughter.

LEA. Oh dear. Tell me. Does it rhyme, Herr Hensel?

WILHELM. It does, I'm afraid, and was written with a *square pencil*.

LEA. No. No no. I understand we're not the rabble you're used to, Herr Hensel, but rhyme is the crime of the pudding-head. Don't say anything, Paul, it was accidental.

PAUL. It wasn't just a poem, was it, Herr Hensel.

LEA. What else?

WILHELM. And, uh, a small sketch.

LEA. That's more like it – of Fanny? Oh, or Felix, perhaps! The latter is the more eye-catching subject, of course.

PAUL. I don't think it was either of them, was it, Herr Hensel?

LEA. Who then? Come, let's see it.

WILHELM. I'd rather not. It is not so good – allow me to hide it in my pocket.

LEA. Your reluctance is setting on my desire!

FELIX *enters*.

FELIX. Mother.

LEA. One moment. Come, show me, perhaps Italy has improved your mettle.

> WILHELM *wavers and then hands over one of two pieces of paper in his hand.* LEA *takes it.*

Let's see now... oh, there's nothing on it!

WILHELM. Perhaps I've *drawn a blank.*

> PAUL *laughs* – LEA *shudders.*

LEA. Paul!

> PAUL *stops laughing.* LEA *scrunches the paper up and throws it into the bin.*

No more games now. Show me. Are you still in the style of Raphael?

> LEA *takes the second piece of paper from him.*

I don't recognise the face.

PAUL. Keep looking.

LEA. Oh!

WILHELM. Allow me to explain –

LEA. It's you!

PAUL. It's him!

LEA. It is improper for a man to offer his portrait to a young girl.[18]

WILHELM. Well, perhaps traditionally speaking, but after five years of separation, a romantic gesture felt important to... to...

> LEA *lets him falter. It's awkward.* FELIX *breaks the awkwardness.*

FELIX. Mother?

LEA. What?

FELIX. Fanny would like a moment with you.

LEA. Of course.

WILHELM. My intentions were –

LEA. I know exactly what your intentions were, Herr Hensel, you're coming on stronger than a garlic-infused Hercules. Excuse me.

LEA is about to exit.

Do something about it, *man*.

LEA exits with the self-portrait.

WILHELM. My apologies, I must be the only painter who needs to *brush up* on his courtship etiquette!

Neither of them laugh.

So Beethoven's not the only composer with deaf ears... Quickly, call a doctor, my sense of humour's dying!... You know, they say that humour –

FELIX. Italy. Did you enjoy much Puccini or Rossini whilst you were there?

WILHELM. I enjoyed plenty of spaghetti.

FELIX. What of Rome?

WILHELM. Ah, Rome, home sweet Rome. A Rome-antic place.

PAUL. Did you sit for any ceremonies at St Peter's?

WILHELM. Oh, a pew.

FELIX. Are you frightened of serious conversation, Herr Hensel? Because my sister is a serious person. She's not ribbon and frills. You're unlikely to compete with the richness of her life if all you can offer is fluff.

WILHELM. What do you mean?

FELIX. I mean that you will need to persuade her to make space for you. If you want her attention you will need to capture it.

WILHELM. From who?

FELIX. Well, Herr Moscheles and Herr Bach at the moment.

WILHELM. Who are they?

PAUL. Her current obsessions.

FELIX. But I use them merely as an example. Yes, they have her heart; they speak to her soul; but they're metonymic of the bounteous arts and enlightened conversations that make up her life here. If you want to be, as you should be, her primary interest then you'll need more than little jokes.[19]

WILHELM. She always liked my little jokes.

FELIX. She's not a girl any more, Herr Hensel. Do you understand?

WILHELM. What about 'to thine own self be true'?

FELIX. Sure, if you want to get stabbed behind an arras! Look. Paul, people hate it when you're yourself, don't they?

PAUL. It's why I'm always trying to be someone else!

WILHELM. What if I just trust my instincts?

FELIX. That's exactly the type of thing you mustn't do.

LEA *enters with* FANNY.

LEA. Herr Hensel, allow me to introduce Frauline Mendelssohn-Bartholdy.

FANNY. You look different.[20]

WILHELM *finds this amusing*.

WILHELM. Hello to you too.

FANNY. Sorry. Hello. I don't remember you so old.

WILHELM. Well... in every moment up until this one I've been younger!

FANNY *finds this amusing*.

FELIX. I shall leave you both to get acquainted.

FANNY. Oh, okay, yes, you must go.

FELIX (*aside to* FANNY). He's a catch, sister. (*To the room.*) Farewell. Farewell, Herr Hensel.

FELIX *exits.*

LEA. Paul, leave us.

PAUL. Certainly.

FANNY. Wait, Paul.

PAUL. Of course.

FANNY *pulls her mother to one side for a quiet moment.*

FANNY. Mother, I feel as if I've swallowed a fistful of butterflies.

LEA. That's to be expected.

FANNY. I care, so much, what you think.

LEA. Of course you do.

FANNY. Speaking to a visitor in front of you feels like playing Bach in front of Bach.

LEA *is disappointed but understanding.*

LEA. Does it?

FANNY. I'd feel more comfortable around someone whose opinion is less important to me.

LEA. I see. You would behave as if I were here though, yes?

FANNY. I promise to.

LEA. Then we must find someone whose opinion is irrelevant. Paul. You're chaperoning.

FANNY. Thank you, Mother.

LEA. I had butterflies once too. Herr Hensel, will you forgive me? I have some correspondences which require urgent attention.

WILHELM. There's nothing to forgive.

LEA. Sweet. Behave.

LEA exits. PAUL settles down with his cello – intending to be present but unobtrusive. Perhaps he plucks/bows something which underscores the scene occasionally.

FANNY. I'm wearing a ribbon in my hair.

WILHELM. Yes. There it is.

FANNY. Mother and I couldn't agree on its colour. She thought it was chestnut but I think it contains shades of russet. You're a painter, what colour would you say it is?

WILHELM. Brown.

FANNY. Oh yes, of course, brown. Do you like it?

WILHELM. It's palettable.

FANNY. A pun, because I said you were a painter!

WILHELM looks anxiously at PAUL, who is curious but pretty much minding his own business.

WILHELM. Sorry, that was an accident.

FANNY. I enjoyed it.

WILHELM. Oh, you did?

FANNY. Do you think the ribbon suits me, Herr Hensel?

WILHELM glances at PAUL again.

WILHELM. Uh, yes.

FANNY. You do?

WILHELM. A normal, moderate amount.

FANNY. I see, yes, perhaps you're right. I shall take it off. It's not very me. I feel like wearing a ribbon is like banging one's head against the piano.

PAUL. I think you're rather good at playing by ear.

This unexpected joke makes FANNY laugh.

WILHELM. I don't follow.

FANNY. Oh. Uh, when we play something without music we say it's playing by ear which I suppose, if taken literally, might look like banging one's head against the piano, I think that's what Paul was getting at. But you're right, Herr Hensel: ribbons are for the like of my mother. Though they do say that I've got nice eyes. Good for a painter, I'm told, the eyes. Would you agree?

WILHELM. I'm not sure what I ought to say.

FANNY. Oh God! Say what you feel, not what you ought to say!

WILHELM. Well, you know they have a saying in Italy? It's rather charming, they say, when they like someone, or find an aspect of someone appealing they say: my compliments to your mother. Do you like that? My compliments to your mother, she must be very dewy-eyed.

FANNY. Herr Hensel!

PAUL. ...Oh Jesus.

FANNY. Well, your mother must be very, very sturdy.

WILHELM. How kind of you to say! Yes! She is!

FANNY. Would you like to paint my eyes, Herr Hensel?

WILHELM. Paint them? I'd like to strip off and swim in them.

FANNY *runs to the piano.* PAUL *catches* WILHELM*'s eye.*

PAUL. I'm still here.

WILHELM. Sorry.

FANNY. Can I play you something?

WILHELM. Of course! I should like that a lot. Like a lot, a lot actually, moderately speaking.

FANNY *moves to the piano and begins riffling through sheet music, talking as she does so.*

FANNY. It's a little reductive – this thing fluttering about in my chest is far more complex than... well, but the way this bounces up the keyboard is – Ah, here it is! You'll see.

WILHELM. You wrote this?

FANNY. Moscheles.

Music: 'Rondo in D-major, Op. 18: No. 2', Moscheles.

PAUL *is watching* WILHELM. WILHELM *sees him looking. It makes him anxious.* WILHELM *interrupts.*

WILHELM. Sorry, I'm sorry, do you mind, uh –

FANNY. What?

WILHELM. Stopping.

FANNY. You don't like it?

WILHELM. Perhaps we could just talk? It would be nice to talk, wouldn't it?

FANNY. I'm not giving a concert, it was folded into our conversation. I'm trying to express something to you that my words are struggling to contain. That's the magic of music.

WILHELM. I do understand the magic of music.

FANNY. Then what?

WILHELM. It's just, I'd like to hear from you, not him.

FANNY. From who?

WILHELM. Him. Showmalez.

FANNY. I don't mean to embarrass you, Herr Hensel, but it's Moscheles.

WILHELM. Does that matter to you – if I get it wrong?

FANNY. I expect it matters to Moscheles.

WILHELM. Enough of him. Why don't you ask me about Italy?

FANNY. I expect I will. When the conversation winds its way there.

WILHELM. I've been away for five years, I come straight to see you, and you haven't asked me a single thing about it. Don't you want to ask about my trip? Ask me something. Go on.

FANNY *bristles – she doesn't like the turn in their conversation.* WILHELM *senses it.*

FANNY. How was Italy, Herr Hensel?

WILHELM. Uh. Sunny.

FANNY. Is that it? You can't speak of conversation then lose your voice. Tell me something interesting about Italy.

WILHELM. Okay. Well… okay, yes, here we go…! Unfortunately I didn't get to enjoy any Puccini or Rossini, but I –

FANNY. Why not?

WILHELM. Why what?

FANNY. You didn't enjoy Puccini or Rossini?

WILHELM. No, but –

FANNY. Do you not like music at all?

WILHELM. No, but I liked the spaghetti!

FANNY. What do you mean?

WILHELM. I didn't enjoy Puccini or Rossini but –

FANNY. I know, Herr Hensel, you've said. You don't like Puccini, Rossini or Moscheles.

WILHELM. Rome! I found it to be a very Rome-antic place.

FANNY. Did you? You'll forgive me for not tugging at that thread.

WILHELM. Oh no – no no no, I'm not suggesting that –

FANNY. Have you a silly poem or something?

WILHELM. I feel as if I've upset you.

FANNY. Where's this poem? You did promise you would bring one.

WILHELM. I did have a poem, it's just, your mother, she's…

FANNY. What?

WILHELM. Well…

FANNY. What?

PAUL. Yes, what?

WILHELM. She took it.

FANNY. Why?

WILHELM. Well, I don't want to be rude but I think because she lacks the romance of the age.

FANNY. So you don't care for my mother and you don't care for music. You should know, Herr Hensel, I like both of those things very much.

WILHELM. I know, it's just, I'm beginning to think I don't understand them – I don't think I understand this house.

FANNY. But you understand that they're important to me.

WILHELM. Of course! But I suppose painting is important to me but I'm not going to marry *The Birth of Venus*. We must make space in our lives for one another.

FANNY. I don't find jealousy very endearing, Herr Hensel.

WILHELM. That's not to say – I adore your work, I do – it's just that –

FANNY. You don't need to justify yourself to me, Herr Hensel. I understand.

There's an awkward moment.

Do you know, I've thought about you almost every day.

WILHELM. And I, you.

FANNY. But I'm not sure I recognise the man in front of me as the man I held in my heart.[21]

WILHELM. Oh. It was very sunny, do you think it's the tan?

FANNY. Do you know, I'm suddenly very tired.

WILHELM. Oh. You are?

FANNY. Yes, I think the anxiety of not knowing the colour of this ribbon has left me exhausted! You must forgive me, Herr Hensel.

WILHELM. Uh, okay, yes, you are forgiven.

FANNY. I mean to say, would you do me the kindness of permitting me a little restful solitude.

WILHELM. Is it something I have said?

FANNY. Not at all, I have just been a little unwell this morning, that is all. Nosebleeds, a little numbness in the extremities, that sort of thing – runs in the family,[22] but it's important to take these things seriously, especially after Father, so I suddenly feel as if I really ought to lay down in a very dark room – permanently.

WILHELM. Oh yes, of course, you must take care of yourself.

FANNY. Thank you, Herr Hensel, you're very considerate.

WILHELM. May I give you something before I go?

FANNY. No thank you.

WILHELM. Can I at least say something – something nice.

FANNY. You've said quite a lot.

WILHELM. Then, may I be permitted to return?

FANNY thinks. She looks at PAUL. She knows what she feels but not what she has to say.

FANNY. It's not my place to say.

WILHELM. Oh…

FANNY. Paul.

PAUL. Yes, of course.

FANNY. Good day, Herr Hensel.

WILHELM. Good day.

WILHELM *and* PAUL *exit.*

FANNY *watches the door for a moment – trying to control herself. She picks up her conductor's baton and brings in the orchestra.*

Music: Les Élémens, simphonie nouvelle, *'1. Le cahos (or 'chaos')', Rebel.*

PAUL *enters. He watches his sister conducting in her head.*

PAUL. Fanny?

The music stops – FANNY *turns to her brother, the pot bubbling.*

I'm sorry to interrupt.

FANNY. What do you need, Paul?

PAUL. I'm the same, I find music cheaper and more effective than drinking a glass of wine.

FANNY. What do you mean?

PAUL. I thought you might be upset.

FANNY. Why would I be upset?

PAUL. Yes, good, I suppose it is ultimately a fate well avoided.

FANNY. In what sense?

PAUL *(teasing her a little).* More time for 'Paul's Theme'?

FANNY. I'm not sure Herr Hensel would approve.

PAUL. What do you mean?

FANNY. You were there, Paul. I'm not sure Herr Hensel has much care for music.

PAUL. You're still considering him?

FANNY. Two opposing notes can be held together in harmonic union.

PAUL. But two notes *held* together is a drone. You really must, at least –

FANNY. What do you know of 'must'? I wager you are more familiar with 'want' than 'must'.

PAUL. I suppose I am.

FANNY. I know you are. I understand 'must'. I've lived a life of 'must'! And let me tell you, Paul, there's no 'must' about this! I am to be a wife. I *want* to be.

They both know it's not true.

PAUL. How about a little 'Paul's Theme'?

FANNY. I'm going upstairs.

PAUL. Maybe I could tell you a secret?

FANNY. I know all your secrets.

PAUL. No you don't! How about this, where did I first –

FANNY. The stables at the Britzer gardens. And it's not a secret, Paul, because they all saw you. Tell Mother I've gone to bed.

FANNY *is about to exit.*

PAUL. Felix played for Queen Victoria, yes?

FANNY. And I'm thrilled for him.

PAUL. He found a volume of his lieder on her piano. He asked the Queen to pick her favourite; and which one did she choose? 'Italien. Italien!' Her favourite of Felix's lieder was *yours*. The Queen's favourite piece of music is *yours*.

FANNY. How could you possibly know that?

PAUL. Mother – Felix put it in writing to her.

FANNY. And they said nothing?

PAUL. They want music to be an ornament in your life.

FANNY. Both of them?

PAUL *lets the silence speak.* FANNY *takes it in.*

PAUL. I may not understand 'must' but I do know what it feels like to be overlooked.

LEA *enters*.

LEA. I knew it! That was Herr Hensel scurrying down the garden path, wasn't it?!

PAUL. It wasn't my fault!

LEA. What did you say to him, Fanny? Paul, run after him!

PAUL. Me?

FANNY. It's what he said to me, Mother. He was different, as you warned he might be.

LEA. He's not converted, you know.

FANNY. That doesn't make him the perfect suitor.

LEA. He's the only suitor. Go and fetch him back, Paul.

PAUL. Why me?

LEA. Allow me to be blunt: Fanny – yes, you're witty and passionate and have interests – but you're getting older. You must school yourself more seriously and more eagerly for your true profession, a young woman's only profession, being mistress of the house![23]

FANNY. I am taking it seriously.

LEA. Then let's fetch him back. Paul!

FANNY. I think you'd be happy if I married a turnip.

PAUL. So long as it was a Lutheran turnip.

LEA. Paul! Go!

PAUL. I don't want to!

LEA. Look, he's interested and he's the right side of thirty! What more do you want?

FANNY. How old is he?

LEA. Thirty-four.

FANNY. How is that the right side of thirty?

PAUL. It's her side of thirty.

LEA. Why are you still here?! GO!!

PAUL. No!

FANNY. Mother, listen to me, I'm not sure that I could grow to love that man.

LEA. *Love*! What, are you a butcher's daughter now?

FANNY. The one liberty I have is to choose a husband.

LEA. Fanny, you are not the great dimwit you're pretending to be. Paul!

PAUL. No!

FANNY. He cares not for music!

LEA. He adores your music – it was practically the first thing he said! Be open, Fanny.

FANNY. I am open!

LEA. Marriage doesn't have to be a punishment. You can still read and socialise and enjoy music as a hobby. Paul, go!

PAUL. How many times! I'm not going!

FANNY. How can you say that?! Queen Victoria likes my work!

PAUL. Okay, I'll go.

FANNY. That's what you said, isn't it, Paul?

PAUL. Fanny…!

LEA. Paul?

FANNY. That's right, isn't it, Paul?

PAUL. Mother, I didn't say a word, I promise.

FANNY. Paul did the right thing. I have a right to know! That's why you told me, isn't it Paul?

PAUL. I, uh, well, I uh, I uh, well, I uh –

The doorbell jingles.

I'll get it! Please let me get it!

FANNY. No, Paul, wait –

LEA. Herr Hensel returns! Thank goodness! Show him in, Paul.

FANNY. Wait, Paul! Please, Mother, please. Don't make me beg. Don't let him up! Please!

LEA. Fanny, stop it.

FANNY. Just not right now. Just say that I'm at lunch! Yes, we could say that I'm at lunch! That's something people do, I think?

LEA. You must take life seriously!

FANNY. Dead! Perhaps I'm suddenly dead!

LEA. No more! You would not be here had I not married with your father, God rest his ginormous forehead. You will entertain Herr Hensel again and that's an end to it. Paul, go.

PAUL *exits. Who's going to speak first...?*

Hands.

FANNY. You didn't tell me.

LEA. It doesn't change anything.

Neither of them enjoy the truth of LEA*'s statement.*

Show me your hands.

FANNY *holds them out.* LEA *looks at them. Very gently she takes* FANNY*'s hands in hers.*

For a moment she seems upset.

Very good. Be doing something ladylike when he returns.

FANNY. What do you suggest?

LEA. Here, read some Shakespeare.

FANNY. Which one?

LEA. It doesn't matter. *The Two Gentlemen of Somewhere, The Merchant of Somewhere Else, Summer's Midnight Dream.* Just look like you enjoy it.

LEA *hands* FANNY *a book.*

FANNY. I like Shakespeare.

LEA. You see, that's the spirit. Show him kindness. I'm sorry, Fanny. This is how it must be.

LEA *exits.* FANNY *waves in the orchestra.*

Music: 'In furore iustissimae irae, RV 626', Vivaldi.

The door opens and she spins around, brightly – the music stopping.

FANNY. Herr Hensel!

PAUL *enters.*

PAUL. It's just me. It was the post.

PAUL *is riffling through the post. His preoccupation allows them to avoid a confrontation.*

Et tu, Fanny?

FANNY (*teasing*). Don't let Mother hear you speaking Latin – she'll think that you've converted.

PAUL. I told you in confidence.

FANNY (*knowing she should apologise*). You kept it from me first.

PAUL. Still, I don't think throwing me to the wolf was the right thing to do.

PAUL *hands out a letter.*

Here, F. Mendelssohn.

PAUL *hands over the letter and tries to exit elegantly but, again, gets his cello stuck in the doorway.*

We need bigger doors.

PAUL *exits.* FANNY *tears the letter open, she sees immediately it's not for her.*

FANNY (*shouting off*). Paul, this is for Felix, it's a –

Something catches her eye.

Con fuoco!

QUEEN VICTORIA *and* PRINCE ALBERT *appear in a spotlight.*

VICTORIA. 'Dear F. Mendelssohn, the great F. Mendelssohn, the one and only F. Mendelssohn! Guess what…? It's Queen Victoria here, you lucky German!'

ALBERT. And Albert.

VICTORIA. Oh yes, and Albert. 'Listen, honeypot, I adored your last visit – I cannot stop thinking about your hands – '

ALBERT. What?

VICTORIA. '– about the ease and dexterity of your hands at my piano! Never mind the piano*forte*, I expect one day they will be calling it the piano*Mendelssohn*!' Albert – laugh.

ALBERT *laughs.*

Eugh.

ALBERT. Do you think they'll ever name anything after me?

VICTORIA. No.

ALBERT. I think my name has a nice ring to it!

VICTORIA. Quiet. 'During your last visit I enjoyed your rendition of '*Italien*' so much – like, *so* so much – that I had to invite my favourite composer to come back to London as soon as ASAP! You must premiere… an orchestral work! At the Royal Palace with our world-class Philharmonic Orchestra! And, toffee-cheeks, you simply must conduct it yourself! Write to us soon!'

VICTORIA *and* ALBERT. 'Yours sincerely!'

VICTORIA *and* ALBERT *disappear.*

FANNY *looks up at the audience/orchestra, breathless. The first phrase of (below) snaps into life:*

Music: The Four Seasons, *'Concerto No. 2 in G-minor, RV 315 "Summer": III. Presto'*, Vivaldi.

Silence. FANNY *looks at the letter again.* VICTORIA *and* ALBERT *appear in a spotlight.*

VICTORIA. 'I had to invite my favourite composer to come back to London as soon as ASAP.'

FANNY *looks up at the audience/orchestra, breathless. The second phrase of (below) plays:*

Music: Vivaldi – The Four Seasons, Concerto No. 2 in G minor, RV 315 'Summer': III. Presto

Silence. FANNY *looks at the letter again.* VICTORIA *and* ALBERT *appear in a spotlight.*

'– my favourite composer –'

FANNY *looks up at the audience/orchestra, breathless. The first third phrase, onwards, of (below) plays:*

Music: The Four Seasons, 'Concerto No. 2 in G-minor, RV 315 "Summer": III. Presto', Vivaldi.

FANNY *races about the room grabbing quills, sheet music, ink!*

She drags a travel case into the room and starts hurling things into it.

FELIX *storms into the room.*

As he SLAMS! the door behind him the music stops.

FELIX. Jollocks! They're malmsey-nosed mutton-shunters, the lot of them!

FANNY. Brother!

FELIX. Utter ratbags!

FANNY. What happened, brother?

FELIX. What happened?

FANNY. Did it not go well?

FELIX. Why did I allow you all to convince me that Berlin has any care for me at all!

FANNY. They didn't give you the post?

FELIX. Of course they didn't!

FANNY. Grell?!

FELIX. No! The blockhead only got four votes.

FANNY. And you?

FELIX. Eighty-eight.

PAUL (*off*). That sounds like quite a lot!

FELIX opens the door to PAUL, *kneeling at the keyhole.*

FELIX. Rungenhangen got one hundred and forty-eight![24]

PAUL. Oh.

FELIX slams the door in PAUL's *face.* PAUL *reopens it and joins the conversation.*

FELIX. One hundred and forty-eight! I have been publicly slapped in the face! Do you know what they did? They offered me the post of assistant director! Assistant director!

FANNY. Brother.

PAUL. Are you taking it?

FELIX. Am I heck! I told them in the politest possible terms that they could go hang themselves![25]

FANNY. They've clearly made a mistake, brother! Rungenhagen's old, he's decrepit, he must be at least fifty-five!

PAUL. Then why him?

FANNY. Because he's the easy choice! It's classic Berlin – stuck in the past! They're just used to him being around all the time, that's the only reason to pick him over you.

FELIX. You're right – Berlin is so inert it's rotting. I'm unappreciated! Well, I am done with Berlin! Paul, pack my bags!

PAUL. I don't do that any more.

FANNY. Where are you going?

FELIX. To England! To where I am appreciated! To where I am understood! Paul!

PAUL. No.

FANNY. You're going to England?

FELIX. Right away! Paul, go pack my bags!

PAUL. Okay, yes I will, but, can I just say, it's because I want to, not because you're shouting at me.

FANNY. Now?

FELIX. And call for a coachman to take me to the station at Potsdamer.

PAUL exits.

FANNY. You're upset – just stay a little – you're not the type of person to –

FELIX. Don't tell me what I am and what I'm not!

FANNY. But, what of you and I, brother?

FELIX. We have sent letters before.

FANNY. Mother won't be happy.

FELIX. Is she ever?

FANNY. Frau Schumann is coming – you must stay and speak to her. And –

FELIX. Argh! You're a church bell! It's not my fault she's late. And, tell me, Fanny, what's the point in hanging around here like death's head upon a mop stick, huh? Excuse me.

FANNY. Brother, I miss you when you're not here!

FELIX. You'll get used to it! Lobcocks!

SLAM! FELIX exits.

FANNY. *Scherzo!*

FANNY quickly grabs a few things and runs for the door.

As she opens it, WILHELM *bursts back into the room.*

WILHELM. Do you like magic?

FANNY. Herr Hensel – !

WILHELM. Hello, yes, sorry, I'm, here I am again –

FANNY. You can't just burst back in here!

WILHELM. Yes, no, sorry about that, it's, I don't make a habit of it, but I think this is actually quite important. Very important.

FANNY. You have to go!

WILHELM. Do you like magic? I mean, do you want to see a magic trick?

FANNY. Can you make yourself disappear?

WILHELM (*nervous laughter*). You're funny. I'm talking about the wonders of the supernatural. Close your eyes.

FANNY. No.

WILHELM. Imagine your future, where you are the happiest you've ever been and there's nothing but sunshine and joyful... fun... hours. The birds are singing – (*He whistles.*) lovely song. And you have everything you've ever wanted. Are you imagining this? Imagine it, really imagine it.

FANNY. No.

WILHELM. Now, open your eyes.

FANNY. They are open.

WILHELM. Ta-dah...!

FANNY. What?

WILHELM. Here I am: the future! Your future! Oh God, why did I think this was a good idea...

FANNY. We've both read books. I understand why you think you're able to walk back into this room unannounced and charm your way into redemption but I'm afraid this is not that kind of story, sir. I need you to leave.

WILHELM. Let me start again. Here, here, some plums I picked on my way back from Rome.

FANNY. Take them with you.

WILHELM. Here, here!

> WILHELM *hands over the plums.* FANNY *discards them.*

FANNY. Herr Hensel, I need you to go! Go!

WILHELM. What?

FANNY. Go, yes, go!

WILHELM. Wait – wait – I understand your resistance, you are ill, you're not feeling well, but I beg you hear me out, I beg you, I beg of you.

FANNY. How many successful courtships have started with begging, do you think?

WILHELM. Press? Is that better? Pressing... I press you?

FANNY. Herr Hensel, I'm going to save us both some time, I could permit you to remain, and the next several hours would be made up of subtle gestures, lingering gazes, well-timed compliments but, at the end of it all, I would still answer no. So shall we just skip to that bit? No. You may go.

WILHELM. Look at me! I couldn't well-time an egg! I don't want to gesture or linger or, I mean look, look here's me whispering – sibilantly – or inclining my head – or gazing –

FANNY. Herr Hensel!

WILHELM. It's just – please may I speak?

FANNY. My answer, sir, is no. Now, please take your leave!

WILHELM. What question are you answering? I haven't asked one!

FANNY. We both know why you have returned, sir.

WILHELM. You cannot answer a question that I have not been allowed to ask!

FANNY. Yes I can!

WILHELM. I must be permitted to ask a question!

FANNY. Here's a question for you. What am I asking you to do?

WILHELM. Leave.

FANNY. And what are you doing?

WILHELM. I'm staying.

FANNY. And what am I asking you to do?

WILHELM. Leave.

FANNY. And what are you doing?

WILHELM. I'm staying.

FANNY. And what am I asking you to do?

WILHELM. Leave.

FANNY. And what are you doing?

WILHELM. I'm staying.

FANNY. And what am I asking you to do?

WILHELM. I know, I know, but I don't understand why!

FANNY. I'm not sure how much clearer I can make it for you. I would rather lick a wasp than say yes to you. I would rather live a life without food or warmth or light or Bach than say yes to you. I'd rather set myself on fire and then drown myself in a lake than say yes to you. The answer is no.

WILHELM. But –

FANNY. No.

WILHELM. If –

FANNY. No.

WILHELM. No?

FANNY. No.

WILHELM. Oh God, is this what I'm asking, I'm not wanting to, but it's coming out now anyway, here it is… are you doing that thing I'm told fashionable young ladies are doing: are you saying no when you mean yes?

FANNY. Oh, Herr Hensel…

WILHELM. I didn't say it! I didn't say it! I – I – I – I'm hot! Are you hot? I feel perhaps we should open a window?

WILHELM *begins taking off his jacket.*

FANNY. I will consent to that, sir, only if you promise that you'll hurl yourself from it!

LEA *enters –* WILHELM *is in a physical pickle and doesn't look ravishing.*

LEA. Herr Hensel, lovely to see you again. You look so ravishing this afternoon you'll make the flowers jealous. Have you been here alone?

WILHELM. Forgive me, Frau Mendelssohn-Bartholdy, it's because I was about to leave.

LEA. Nonsense! Fanny, what have you said?

FANNY. Nothing, Mother!

WILHELM. Uh… It was my idea, Frau Mendelssohn-Bartholdy.

LEA. Well, you are forgiven, Herr Hensel. Not all ideas are good ones! Fanny, you don't wish Herr Hensel to leave, do you?

FANNY. Of course not.

LEA. You see!

WILHELM. You don't?

FANNY. But, Mother, I have no wish to hold Herr Hensel here against his will.

LEA. Come, Fanny, what have I told you: men have no real will of their own! Do you, Herr Hensel?

WILHELM. Uh...

LEA. You see what I mean! Men like to be treated like grapes.

WILHELM. We do?

LEA. Stamped on until you resemble something the lady would like to have with dinner. You will stay, Herr Hensel. Fanny, you want him to stay.

FANNY. Of course, but I can see you're already reaching for the door handle, Herr Hensel.

WILHELM. So it is your wish for me to go?

LEA. No, not at all.

FANNY. But I have no wish to stop you doing what you want to do.

WILHELM. Then you would have me go.

FANNY. Yes.

LEA. Fanny!

WILHELM. You would?

FANNY. If that is what he wants.

WILHELM. In good earnest?

FANNY. Of course. You must do what you want.

WILHELM. I see.

FANNY. And I'm sure you will have a splendid time being *somewhere else*.

WILHELM. Then I will go.

FANNY. I'm sorry to hear that.

WILHELM. Then I will stay.

FANNY. But it will be a pleasure for you to leave, I imagine.

LEA. Fanny!

FANNY. Herr Hensel, do you or do you not want to go?

WILHELM. I want to go only to please you.

FANNY. Pardon, Herr Hensel, I didn't quite catch that.

WILHELM. I want to go –

FANNY. So it is your want to go! I knew it! How cruel to say it so unambiguously!

WILHELM. Cruel?

FANNY (*playing up for her mother*). You clearly have no interest in me – you have just said as much! If you 'want to go' as you have just said you do, then you must! Go!

WILHELM. Then I will! At this very moment I will give you your wish.

FANNY. Very well.

WILHELM. *Your* wish.

LEA. It is not her wish!

FANNY. It is if that is what *you* wish.

WILHELM. *You're* going to get exactly what *you* wish.

FANNY. I wish none of this was happening.

WILHELM. I will take my leave of you!

> WILHELM *moves towards the door* – FANNY *follows him to close the door behind him* – *he turns back*.

I will follow the course you've laid out for me.

> FANNY *says nothing*. WILHELM *moves towards the door* – FANNY *follows him* – *he turns back*.

I will embark on the path as you've described it.

> FANNY *says nothing*. WILHELM *is in the hallway now. He turns back*.

I will fly from here like –

> *SLAM!* FANNY *shuts the door in his face.*

FANNY. Don't say it, Mother. He clearly wanted to go!

WILHELM *enters*.

WILHELM. I didn't want to go! I want to stay, I have something I need to say.

LEA. Yes, yes, speak, listen. Go on.

WILHELM. Courtship is not the reason I came back.

LEA. What?

WILHELM. I am entirely unmusical. And, I meant what I said, I don't think I do understand this house, this world you're in –

FANNY. Herr Hensel –

WILHELM. In that – I just mean to say that I simply can't speak this foreign language you're all so fluent in.

FANNY. Herr Hensel –

WILHELM. But – but – I came here because I wanted to give you something. Something I've wanted to give you all day.

LEA. What a thoughtful and good-natured man Herr Hensel is, to bring a token of his affection!

WILHELM *reaches into the bin*.

Oh God, he's rummaging about in the bin.

WILHELM *pulls out a crumpled piece of paper and flattens it out*.

WILHELM. Here.

LEA *grabs it*.

LEA. You're giving my beautiful daughter a blank sheet of paper you've pulled from the bin?

WILHELM. Yes.

LEA. Why don't you and your piece of paper run back to your carriage and come back with something that a right-minded suitor would consider a gift.

WILHELM. I can't run back to the carriage.

LEA. Why not?

WILHELM. Because paper is stationery!

LEA. Oh god...

FANNY. Mother, you know that Felix is leaving? He's going back to England.

LEA. No he isn't.

FANNY. He didn't get the job! He's leaving any minute!

LEA. Where is he?

FANNY. Packing! He's called for a carriage! Talk to him!

LEA. But... what about the panting Romeo?

WILHELM. Consider me a sexless amoeba.

LEA. Fine!

LEA *exits*. WILHELM *takes the piece of paper from* LEA *as she passes and holds it out to* FANNY.

FANNY. What do you mean by this?

WILHELM. This is what I think of you.

FANNY. Nothing?

WILHELM. Possibility. I might not understand music as a creator, or performer, but I couldn't leave your house thinking that I had done or said anything that misrepresented how I feel when I hear your music. It's... My art is temporal, fleshy, a nose is nose, an eye an eye, a tooth –

FANNY. – a tooth?

WILHELM. A tooth! But your work is celestial. Of course I didn't convert to the Catholic Church in Italy. The only thing I've ever truly believed in is you.

FANNY. Herr Hensel –

WILHELM. And that's not to say we must be together – I would die to think I was making you do something that you'd rather not – but, you must keep taking empty pages like this one and filling it with... you. Because, though you are beautiful, and kind, and though I'd like you to be my wife, a mother even – that will never be all that you are.

FANNY. Herr Hensel –

WILHELM. And I promise, I will happily bring you an empty piece of paper every day, for as long as I live, if you promise to keep filling it.[26] Here is today's.

WILHELM *hands* FANNY *the paper – she takes it.*

I've finished.

FANNY *is deadly serious and unsmiling.*

I see. Okay. Farewell.

WILHELM *is about to exit.*

FANNY. Wait.

WILHELM. What?

FANNY. I think, perhaps, you should come again tomorrow. With another piece of paper.

WILHELM. Is that something that you want?

FANNY. I don't know...

WILHELM. That's understandable.

FANNY. My brother has to run off to England to find appreciation but I have it right here – (*Waves the piece of paper.*) – why would I go anywhere else? Yes, it is something that I want. Come tomorrow. This has brought me happiness, *Wilhelm Hensel*.

WILHELM. And that's all I want, *Fanny Mendelssohn*.

FANNY. Perhaps my happiness will grow each day.

WILHELM. I hope that too!

FANNY. My compliments to your mother – she must've been a work of art.

WILHELM *is a bit confused.*

I think you have a pleasing face.

WILHELM. I do?

FANNY. You do.

WILHELM. Would you like to walk in the garden?

FANNY. Very much. I just need to give something to my brother.

FELIX *enters looking for his 'Wedding March' – he sees it on the piano.*

FELIX. Ah, here it is.

FANNY. Brother!

FELIX *is on his way out of the room to continue packing.*

FELIX. I'm going to stop you, Fanny – Mother's already tried.

FANNY. No, I have good news for you brother.

FELIX. Oh! Allow me to shake your hand, Herr Hensel! Congratulations!

WILHELM. Uh, thank you.

FANNY. No. The congratulations are yours, brother!

FELIX. I played a minor role in the courtship, but thank you, sister, it's always nice to be recognised for one's contributions! I'll write something for the big day.

He's about to exit.

FANNY. Felix, you're not listening. I have something to give you. Here.

FANNY *holds out the invitation.* FELIX *is getting ready and doesn't pay attention.*

FELIX. Now is not the time for sharing new work. Besides, your new union forebodes the end of ours.

FANNY. Why does it?

FELIX. Because you're embarking on one of life's great joys! You'll not have time to think of music until your primary activities have been carried out[27] – your house, Herr Hensel, the family. You've found your place! And that's wonderful!

FANNY. I thought my place was to be in your pocket, brother.

FELIX. If I were married and had a husband to coddle and a family around me, I'd be exactly the same, I wouldn't want to be writing scores.[28]

FANNY. One day I'd like to publish work –

FELIX. You are published.

FANNY. Under my name, not yours –

FELIX. These things are only to be done if one intends to present oneself, and remain, as a composer throughout one's life.

FANNY. That is my intention.

FELIX. A composer surely isn't your intention?

FANNY. Of course it is!

FELIX. Then where is your succession of works?

FANNY. I have written consistently – you have taken much of it yourself!

FELIX. Yes, but there must be one after the other after the other. Where is your intent? You have presented a few isolated works – you do not take yourself seriously as a musician.

FANNY. I happen to construe my persistence, with a total lack of external encouragement, as proof of my intent!

FELIX. It proves your circumstance. Wilhelm?

WILHELM. Yes?

FELIX. Have you nothing to say? You can see that Fanny displays neither the wish nor the vocation to be a serious musician.

WILHELM. She is well respected.

FELIX. By me.

FANNY. By others too.

FELIX. In Berlin living rooms, perhaps.

WILHELM. I think it's possible for her to be more than just one thing.

FELIX. What a cruel idea to put into her head, Herr Hensel. Fanny, reconcile yourself to your primary activity in life. It will be joyful!

FELIX is about to exit.

FANNY. What of Queen Victoria?

FELIX. What of her?

FANNY. You said that she likes your work.

FELIX. She *adores* my work.

FANNY. Was there something in particular she liked?

FELIX. One of my lieders.

FANNY. One of *yours*?

FELIX understands the implication.

FELIX. I am such an influence on your compositions, Fanny, that what comes from you is as much a part of me.

FELIX waits a moment to see if FANNY is going to challenge him. Eventually...

Excuse me.

FELIX exits.

FANNY. *Scherzo!* Wilhelm, where's that bit of paper?

PART ONE 57

WILHELM. Here.

> WILHELM *hands it over.* FANNY *begins furiously scribbling on it.*

You're composing?

FANNY. Writing a letter. I need you to go and post it. Immediately. Can you do that?

WILHELM. Of course. To who? Whom? Who? I don't know if…

FANNY. Nobody does. Here, read this.

> FANNY *hands* WILHELM *the invitation. He starts reading it.* FANNY *gathers her things.*

> QUEEN VICTORIA *and* PRINCE ALBERT *appear in a spotlight – they speak a little slower than before.*

VICTORIA. 'Dear F. Mendelssohn, the great F. Mendelssohn, the one and only F. Mendelssohn!'

> FANNY *has her arms full of things.*

FANNY. Where's your carriage?

WILHELM. Outside. Are you taking it?

FANNY. Aren't you coming with me?

WILHELM. Of course. Where?

FANNY. There. Read that bit. Quickly. I'll be back in a moment.

> QUEEN VICTORIA *and* PRINCE ALBERT *speak at double speed.*

VICTORIA. 'Never mind the piano*forte*, I expect one day they will be calling it the piano*Mendelssohn*!' Albert – laugh.

ALBERT *laughs.*

Eugh.

'During your last visit I enjoyed your rendition of '*Italien*' so much – like, *so* so much – that I had to invite my favourite composer to come back to London as soon as ASAP! You must premiere… an orchestral work! At the Royal Palace with our world-class Philharmonic Orchestra! And, toffee-cheeks, you simply must conduct it yourself! Write to us soon!'

VICTORIA *and* ALBERT. 'Yours sincerely!'

VICTORIA *and* ALBERT *disappear.*

FANNY *re-enters with* CLARA SCHUMANN.

FANNY. Look who I found! Frau Schumann, this is Herr Hensel.

CLARA. I like your tie.

WILHELM. Thank you!

FANNY. You've read it? We'll go together?[29]

WILHELM. Yeah! I mean, I'd genuinely love that! When?

FANNY. Post my reply. We'll go as soon as you're back.

WILHELM. Wow.

FANNY. What?

WILHELM. I'm vibrating!

CLARA. You're going on a trip?

FANNY. Sort of. Here – take your fruit with you.

WILHELM. You keep it – it's a metaphor.

FANNY. What do you mean?

WILHELM. Fanny Mendelssohn, my plums are firmly in the palms of your hands!

WILHELM *exits.*

CLARA. He's funny.[30]

FANNY *is moving to the door to shout for her brother whilst keeping the semblance of politeness.*

FANNY. He is. I enjoyed your concert last winter. FELIX! How was your journey?

CLARA. The carriage was like buh-bubuh-bubuh-bubuh, you know?

FANNY (*half-listening*). Oh, yeah, that's the worst. FELIX! He'll be here in a moment. How is Robert?

FANNY *begins slyly gathering things to leave.*

CLARA. There's something in his heart, you know?

FANNY. That's nice.

CLARA. I think it's a fugue. He fell into the Rhine.[31]

FANNY. Oh.

CLARA. Fell... jumped... either way, you know, it was wet.

FANNY. Is he okay?

CLARA. Have you heard of Endenich? It's a sort of hospital.

FANNY. Clara...!

CLARA. I'm fine, I'm fine. Ba-ding! (*Smiles through the pain.*) And they won't let me see him. And it turns out these things are expensive, you know?

FELIX *enters.* CLARA *immediately, deliberately, brightens.*

FELIX. Clara!

CLARA. Felix!

FELIX. Hello.

CLARA. Hello.

FELIX. You look like the jammiest bit of the jam.

CLARA. Says the man who is bang up to the elephant.

FELIX *is thrilled at the complement – he almost doesn't know what to say.*

FANNY. Brother –

FELIX. So you've written something?

CLARA *holds out the score with a little mouth-trumpet fanfare.*

CLARA. Perfect for the director of the Sing-Akademie – I hope!

FELIX. Oh... I withdrew.

CLARA. Your letters suggested –

FELIX. I know, I know, but I'm wasted here in Berlin!

FANNY grabs her brother's arm.

FANNY (*aside to* FELIX). Did she say that you've been sending letters?

FELIX (*aside to* FANNY). A bit. (*To* CLARA.) Don't worry though, we shall find somewhere else to premiere your work.

CLARA. So you will premiere it?

FELIX. You're right – we must hear it first! Come, play, the piano is yours.

CLARA goes to the piano. FANNY grabs FELIX.

FANNY. Felix – !

FELIX. Do you think she'd come to England with me?

FANNY. She's married, brother.

FELIX. And yet, here she is!

FANNY looks at her brother in disbelief.

FANNY. Uh, Jenny Lind!

FELIX. This is nothing like the situation with Jenny Lind.[32]

CLARA has settled at the piano.

CLARA. I'm ready.

FELIX. Play!

CLARA begins playing her concerto. FANNY paces about behind them both, unsure of what to do.

FANNY gets an idea. She catches CLARA's eye. She points at the invitation and gestures 'Shhh/it's a secret' to CLARA. CLARA, confused, begins playing more quietly. FANNY, confused, shakes her head and repeats the actions, trying to emphasise that the letter is 'Shh'. CLARA, *still confused, only really understands the 'Shh' element and plays even more quietly.*

FANNY *waves off what* CLARA *is doing,* CLARA *continues playing at the same volume.*

FANNY *changes tack – she opens the letter and acts 'big news/mind blown/gobsmacked'.* CLARA *plays suddenly very, very loudly and bombastically. It takes* FANNY *and* FELIX *by surprise! Their shock surprises* CLARA.

FANNY, *wary of being rumbled, tells* CLARA *to stop making a scene – she does this by employing a 'calm' double hand/pressing gesture.* CLARA, *immediately dropping to a normal volume, interprets the 'calm' hand gesture as an instruction to slow down.*

FANNY *notices her slowing down.* FANNY *tests her theory. She continues the gesture and* CLARA *continues slowing down.* FANNY *tries something else. With her right hand she conducts* CLARA *to speed up.* CLARA *does so.* FANNY *understands what's happening. She thinks for a moment... she has a plan.*

FANNY *points at* FELIX *and conducts* CLARA *to be aggressive and emphatic with big crunchy voicings.*

CLARA *does so.*

Then, FANNY *conducts* CLARA *to be very narrow and indicates that she should pick up the tempo and play with staccato and be bouncy.* FANNY *mimes running out of the house to this music.*

Then FANNY *thinks... uh...*

She doesn't know exactly what to do so she just mimes getting on a horse and riding it.

CLARA*'s playing takes on a horse-like quality.* FANNY *is surprised and pleased.*

FANNY picks up the pace of her instructions.

FANNY suggests CLARA should be legato *and swirling and florid – FANNY mimes sailing across the sea.*

Then, FANNY brings CLARA right down. FANNY mimes looking around.

As FANNY thinks she sees what she's looking for, the music swells and falls, swells and falls; swells and falls.

Then, FANNY sees the Queen. She gradually conducts CLARA to be bigger, grander, over-the-top and emphatic. CLARA does so – with big juicy chords and rich harmonies and twiddly accents. FANNY, still conducting, mimes a crown on her head – maybe even giving the royal wave.

CLARA, *understanding, suddenly breaks into 'Rule Britannia'.*

FANNY *celebrates then immediately panics.* FELIX *is baffled.*

FELIX. What?!

CLARA stops playing for a second.

CLARA. Uhhh…

CLARA plays two concluding chords.

FELIX. Well, Clara, that was very… eccentric. I've had an idea! Would you like to come to England with me?

CLARA. You'll premiere it in England?

FELIX. Maybe.[33] But there are other things we could do together too.

CLARA. Okay! Yes! Thank you!

FANNY. Clara…!

The doorbell jingles.

I'll get it.

FELIX. We can get it on our way out.

FANNY. I'LL GET IT!

> FANNY *exits and then immediately re-enters.*

It's Robert!

FELIX. What?

CLARA. What?

> CLARA *runs towards the door.*

FANNY. No, no, you mustn't go – he's incandescent with rage.

FELIX. He is? Why?

FANNY. Uh, his fists are full of letters.

FELIX. Our letters?

CLARA. We said nothing.

FANNY. And yet, probably everything!

FELIX. What?

FANNY. You have a reputation, brother.

FELIX. But I'm innocent!

FANNY. He must've read between the lines!

FELIX. I'll talk to him.

FANNY. But Robert's not well, is he, Clara?

CLARA. He's in hospital.

FANNY. He's incarcerated.

FELIX. Is that true?

CLARA. He must have broken free.

FANNY. He may kill you, brother!

FELIX. No! Would he…?

FANNY. Do you mean, have men committed heinous acts in the name of love?

FELIX. I signed the letters 'F. Mendelssohn'. Just tell him it was you!

FANNY. Me?

FELIX. I've got too much to offer the world!

FANNY. But, brother, what comes from me is as much a part of you.

FELIX. What am I going to do?

FANNY. What are you going to do?

FELIX. I could run? Could I run?

CLARA. Let me talk to him!

FANNY. Clara, the red mist has descended!

FELIX. Help me, Fanny, help me!

FANNY. Wait… It's small, but I suppose one of you could hide in this trunk?

FELIX. Yes, yes, brilliant, I'll hide in the trunk!

FELIX clambers in very quickly.

CLARA. What of me?

FELIX. You'll… Good luck.

FELIX closes the lid down on top of himself.

CLARA. Fanny, help me, we haven't – I promise –

FANNY gestures for CLARA to be calm.

FANNY (*whispered*). It's not Robert.

CLARA. It's not –

FANNY gestures 'SHHHHHH!!!'

My heart is like buhbuh-buhbuh-buhbuh-buh.

FANNY (*whispered*). I'm sorry – I had to.

CLARA gives FANNY a quizzical face.

(*Acting.*) I'm sorry, Clara, there's nothing for it! I shall have to let the brute in before he breaks down the door!

FANNY *bangs on the door. The trunk whimpers.*

CLARA *is confused.* FANNY *points at* CLARA *and gestures 'No, no, don't do it!'*

CLARA (*acting*). No, no, don't do it!

FANNY (*whispered*). My brother wants more from you than just your music. Here. Read this.

FANNY *hands* CLARA *the invitation.*

CLARA *takes the invitation and starts reading as* FANNY *goes to the door.*

QUEEN VICTORIA *and* PRINCE ALBERT *appear in a spotlight – they speak a little louder than before.*

VICTORIA. 'Dear F. Mendelssohn, the great F. Mendelssohn –'

FANNY *runs back to* CLARA *waving her hands – 'SHHHH!!!'*

FANNY (*whispered*). Read it quietly! Come with me. To London. We'll add some Decker for you to play. Read, read!

CLARA *nods understandingly.* FANNY *exits as* CLARA *reads quietly.*

QUEEN VICTORIA *and* PRINCE ALBERT *speak at a whisper.*

VICTORIA. 'It's Queen Victoria here, you lucky German!'

CLARA *skims down the page.*

CLARA. Blah-blah-blah-blah-blah...

VICTORIA. Albert – laugh.

ALBERT *laughs.*

CLARA. Blah-blah-blah-blah-blah...

VICTORIA. 'I had to invite my favourite composer to come back to London as soon as ASAP!'

CLARA. Oh my!

VICTORIA. 'And, toffee-cheeks, you can conduct it yourself! Write to us soon!'

VICTORIA *and* ALBERT. 'Yours sincerely!'

VICTORIA *and* ALBERT *disappear.* CLARA *puts the invitation down on the end of the piano.*

FANNY *enters with* WILHELM – *he's a little confused.*

WILHELM. Hello, I am Robert Schumann?

CLARA *beginning to understand, gestures: 'lower, lower'.*

(*Deeper voice.*) I am Robert Schumann.

FANNY *gestures: 'angry'.*

And I am very angry!

FANNY *gestures to* CLARA: *'scream!'*

CLARA *screams.*

CLARA. Robert, unhand me! You beast! You horrible beast!

FANNY *gives her the thumbs-up!*

WILHELM. I am a beast!

FANNY *gives* WILHELM *a 'so-so' gesture.*

FANNY *waves them to carry on as she runs about the room shoving things into her bag.*

CLARA. How did you know I was here? I never should have told you that I was coming here at precisely this moment! What are you looking for? Felix? He's not here! Don't look behind the curtains – he's not there!

WILHELM *thumps over to the curtains, grunting.*

He's not under the piano either!

WILHELM *thumps over to the piano and hits the keys.*

FANNY. Hey!

WILHELM. Sorry... (*Deep.*) Sorry!

CLARA. What? The big trunk in the middle of the room? He's not there, get away from it!

WILHELM *thumps over to the trunk.*

CLARA *and* WILHELM *shake the trunk a little bit.*

FANNY *has finished packing. She gestures to everyone that they're about to go.*

FANNY. Robert, I promise that my brother is – (*Shouts into the trunk.*) not in this trunk. Look!

FANNY *thumps the trunk really hard.* FELIX *screams from inside the trunk.*

Maybe he's hiding in the garden – why don't you go outside and look there?

WILHELM. I will stay here.

FANNY. Okay, Robert, you stay here and keep looking in this room and the rest of us will go.

FANNY, WILHELM *and* CLARA *head towards the door.*

FANNY. Goodbye, Robert!

CLARA. Goodbye!

LEA *enters.*

LEA. Where are you going, amoeba? Are you taking my daughter from the house, Herr Hensel?!

FANNY. Herr Hensel? He's not in this room.

FANNY *looks panicked. She makes the sound of a jingling bell...*

Oh, that'll be him.

LEA. What are you talking about?

FANNY. It's... an idea for an opera.

FANNY *makes the sound of a jingling bell...*

(*Singing.*) I'm coming!

FANNY *sings the thud-thud-thud-thud of footsteps getting further away.*

Then, she does the thud-thud-thud-thud of footsteps getting closer.

She does the squeak of a door – like a mezzo soprano.

(*Singing.*) Come in! Come in and say hello.

FANNY *gestures to* WILHELM.

WILHELM (*singing, badly*). Oh, hello, everyone. Hello, Frau Mendelssohn-Bartholdy.

LEA. What?

WILHELM (*singing, badly*). Fraulein Mendelssohn-Bartholdy.

FANNY (*singing*). Hello, hello, hello.

WILHELM (*singing, badly*). Hello Frau Schumann!

CLARA (*coloratura soprano line*). Hello.

It's such a good soprano line that WILHELM *applauds.*

LEA. I think that's enough.

FANNY *stops* WILHELM *applauding.*

LEA. Fanny, is that your trunk?

FANNY. What do you mean?

LEA. Why is there a travel trunk in the music room?

FANNY *doesn't know what to say.*

Open it.

FANNY. I can't.

LEA. What's inside?

FANNY. Nothing.

LEA. Then open it!

PART ONE 69

FANNY. I can't.

LEA. You're hiding something!

FANNY. No I'm not.

LEA. Then open it and show me what's inside!

FANNY. There's nothing inside it!

The sound of a very nervous fart comes from the trunk.

...Pardon me.

LEA. I demand an explanation! Immediately!

WILHELM. Let me tell you what's going on. I am an artist, Frau Mendelssohn, and I am *drawn* to your daughter, without her I feel *sketchy* and *blue*.

LEA. What are you doing?

WILHELM. I know you are a banking dynasty but I didn't realise Fanny would keep all of my *interest*.

LEA. Stop that at once!

WILHELM. I fear your daughter may be a magician, Frau Mendelssohn.

LEA. Oh God, don't say it.

WILHELM. Because when I look at her *everyone else disappears*!

LEA. I don't feel so well.

WILHELM. I came back from Italy with no money and no pasta – I was penne-less.

LEA. No more!

WILHELM. I was like a duck at a restaurant, telling them to put everything on my bill!

LEA. I can't...

WILHELM. I felt like a fallen horse – I couldn't giddy-up. Or a dog whose day was always ruff.

LEA. A bucket! Get me a bucket!

WILHELM. I thought, in this enlightened and intelligent home, you'd all treat me like a fake noodle!

LEA. Please, Herr Hensel –

WILHELM. An im-pasta! And I know that Fanny wasn't keen on me to start, but I used to hate facial hair…

LEA. You wouldn't…

WILHELM. …but then it grew on me! And I might not trust trees – they're shady – or stairs – they're up to something – or, what about rope, I hear you ask? I'm a frayed knot!

LEA. I can't breathe!

WILHELM. And though I don't have the patients to be a doctor, I'm always two-tyred to unicycle, and periodically wrong to be a scientist –

LEA. The door, the door! Somebody open the door!

FANNY *opens the door.*

WILHELM. But I know that it all changed when I met my encyclopaedia.

LEA. Don't do it…

WILHELM. She contains everything I've been searching for.

LEA. AH!

WILHELM. Because she's Fanny and I'm Willy and by all accounts that's a perfect fit!

LEA. Out of the way!

LEA *charges out of the room as if she's going to be sick.*

FANNY *slams the door shut and runs and embraces* WILHELM.

FANNY. That was brilliant! You're brilliant!

WILHELM. I am?

FANNY. Hey, Wilhelm… you're lucky I'm not a melon.

WILHELM. Why?

FANNY. Or I'd have to say that I cantaloupe.

WILHELM and FANNY giggle.

CLARA. People!

FANNY switches back into business mode.

FANNY. Right. Let's all go and look for Felix outside.

WILHELM (*as* 'Robert'). I am staying in the house until Felix appears.

FANNY. Okay, fine, bye.

FANNY grabs her baton and waves in the orchestra.

A timpani roll creeps in as:

FANNY, CLARA and WILHELM collect the last few things from the room and then run out of it.

SLAM! There's a moment of stillness. Then…

A door swings open. Behind it, on his knees as though he's been listening at the keyhole is… PAUL.

He leaps up and runs into the room.

PAUL. Quick, quick, quick, quick…

He empties the bin. looking for the invitation – nothing!

Quick, quick, quick…

He runs around, looking under cushions, moving books, behind curtains – nothing!

Then… he sees it on the end of the piano. He runs at it, snatches it, and begins reading it.

Quick, quick, quick!

He releases FELIX *from the trunk. He opens a door and drags* LEA *into the room.*

They gather, downstage-centre, and furiously read the letter. The timpani roll explodes into:

Music: Requiem, 'II. Dies irae', Verdi.

On the first four crotchets in the first two bars, the group looks between one another and the audience.

Silence.

FELIX. FANNY!

The music smashes back in! LEA, FELIX *and* PAUL *career around the stage preparing to follow* FANNY.

The music swells and envelops the entire theatre.

Blackout.

Interval.

PART TWO

FANNY *stands centre-stage – it's dark and smoky.*

She waves her baton. A strange sound. Another wave, another strange sound.

Gradually the sounds build and we hear the music of a steam train departing Potsdamer for Hamburg.

As the train sounds swell, a carriage window appears with WILHELM *and* CLARA *inside.*

It makes its way across the stage and collects our conductor.

We see FANNY, CLARA *and* WILHELM *travel across Germany!*

They look out of the window, play games, fall asleep...

Eventually, the train arrives in Hamburg and they run from the carriage towards the docks.

The Docks

BOATSWAIN. Ding-a-ling, ding-a-ling, here's the thing, ding-a-ling, this tink-a-ling, ding-a-ling ding-a-ling, denotes you see, the boats all at sea, ding-a-ling, or to be, you see, clear-cut, ding-a-ling, the port is shut. The port is shut!
Ding-a-ling-ding-a-ling, ding-a-leck...
ding-a-leck... ding-a-leck,
ding-a-lell, ding-a-lell,
I need a new bell,
ding-a-ling, I hate this thing, ding-a-ling-ding-a-ling.

FANNY, CLARA *and* WILHELM *charge onto stage.*

FANNY. London, sir, that's where we're en route to.

BOATSWAIN. Ooooh, well, and hello to you too.

FANNY. I'm sorry, sir, excuse me...
have you had a nice day?

BOATSWAIN. Don't just do it to amuse me!
Look – you see that there's no light?
That means we're shut up for the night.

FANNY. There's nothing till the morning?

BOATSWAIN. Nope.
You'll have to take a pause before elope.

FANNY. Before elope?

BOATSWAIN. That's what I said.
Now move along – it's late, I want my bed.

FANNY. You know you're speaking kinda funny.

BOATSWAIN. I know, I'm a poet – I do boats for the money.

FANNY. Don't be rhyming with me! (*To* WILHELM.) My love?

BOATSWAIN. You need to go elsewhere – please move!

FANNY. What do we do...? Wait – did you just rhyme love and move?

BOATSWAIN. It's a visual rhyme, it's very common.

CLARA. Oh really? I've never heard of that!

BOATSWAIN. Oh, everyone's a critic.

WILHELM. Look – there's a tavern over there.

BOATSWAIN. Men only though – yeah, I know, unfair.

FANNY. We're going now, okay, but we'll see you in the morning, *matey*.

BOATSWAIN. Yeah, great, whatever! I can't... waity.

FANNY, CLARA *and* WILHELM *wince a little.*

I'm trying my best!
Go on then! Go find somewhere to rest.

FANNY, CLARA *and* WILHELM *rush off towards the tavern.*

The Tavern

LANDLADY *enters with a tray of drinks and sings a song about beer.*

In the back of the tavern are two men playing cards seated around a barrel being used as a table.

As FANNY, CLARA (*dressed as men*) *and* WILHELM *rush into the tavern the room falls silent.*

MAN 1, MAN 2 *and* LANDLADY *look at them.*

FANNY *and* CLARA *tentatively tear some fur from a stuffed ferret and stick on fake moustaches.*

That's enough to convince the tavern – everyone goes back to normal!

FANNY. Right, what's your name gonna be?

CLARA. I'll be Bobby. You?

FANNY. I'll be Sebastian.

WILHELM. I'm Eric.

FANNY. No, you're you, Wilhelm, you don't need another name. Eugh, how does anyone compose these things on their face!

WILHELM. You know, you almost look like Felix.

FANNY. Is it the facial hair or the fact I'm passing off someone else's trousers as my own?

LANDLADY *walks past*.

Excuse me –

LANDLADY. Men only.

FANNY. We are men. (*A bit lower*.) We are men. Three men. You have beds?

LANDLADY. Yes.

FANNY. Are they clean beds?

LANDLADY. Fairly clean. We had a group of trombonists in last night. And, well, I'm sure you can imagine. We've only just stuck that bench back together with fish glue! It's sticky – DON'T SIT ON IT! You want the beds?

FANNY. Yes, fine, thank you.

LANDLADY. Three marks.

FANNY. Wilhelm. Wilhelm? Wilhelm! Eric.

WILHELM. Yes?

FANNY. Would you mind collecting some money from the carriage?

WILHELM. Of course.

WILHELM *exits*.

FANNY. One moment.

LANDLADY *exits*.

Clara, what do you think of this?

FANNY *hands some sheet music to* CLARA.

Eugh, I can't concentrate with this thing on my lip.

FANNY *tears off her fake moustache*.

This bit…

She and CLARA *stand in front of the imaginary orchestra and listen.*

Music: 'Overture in C-major', Fanny Mendelssohn.

The music cuts out at the end before bar 186.

And then, I don't know –

CLARA. Let me see it again.

They look at the sheet music again.

Music: 'Overture in C-major', Fanny Mendelssohn.

The music cuts out at the end before bar 186.

Just as the music cuts out, MAN 2 *rather dramatically plays his final card.*

He gives an ascending glissando *of 'Oooooooooooooh'!*

On seeing the card, MAN 1 *thumps the barrel five times.*

FANNY. That's it! A swell of timpani.

CLARA. And then *tutto staccato*?

FANNY. Yes! Look, look.

FANNY *quickly scribbles in her score.*

Like this.

Music: 'Overture in C-major', Fanny Mendelssohn.

This time, CLARA *makes the noise of the music swell and* FANNY *vocalises the timpani beats.*

It works! CLARA *laughs in the rhythm: semiquaver, dotted-quaver, semiquaver, crochet.*

CLARA. Ha-ha ha-HA!

FANNY. Yes, Clara, do that again.

CLARA. What?

FANNY. Ha-ha ha-HA!

CLARA. Laugh?

FANNY. Ha-ha ha-HA!

CLARA. Ha-ha ha-HA!

FANNY. Yes, that's it!

FANNY starts scribbling – LANDLADY has entered with their keys and has overheard.

LANDLADY. Keys. Quite a feminine laugh you've got there, sir.

CLARA. I had something stuck in my throat. I usually laugh down here. (*Octave lower.*) Ha-ha ha-HA!

FANNY. That's better – we should alternate octaves!

FANNY scribbles.

LANDLADY. Where's your moustache gone?

FANNY. I shaved it off.

LANDLADY. In the time it took me to get your keys?

FANNY. Yes.

LANDLADY. With what?

FANNY. I'm ravenous! Do you happen to have some food that we can pay you lots of money for?

LANDLADY. We got chicken or beef.

FANNY. How is the beef?

LANDLADY. It's just like me, sir.

FANNY. Surprisingly tender?

LANDLADY. Tough and old.

FANNY. We'll take three chickens.

LANDLADY. That's five marks and one pfennig.

FANNY. Send our order to the kitchen. My friend will be back any moment with your money.

LANDLADY. Alright, but he'd better be quick!

LANDLADY exits.

FANNY. Okay, so the phrase will alternate over the octaves.

FANNY *conducts here and* CLARA: *'Ha-ha ha-HA!'* (*low*), *'Ha-ha ha-HA!'* (*high*) *x 3*.

And then I think it'll go: BUH! Bubbaduh bubbaduh bubbaduh bubbaduh – buh buh buh buh buh BUH!

Right on cue, MAN 2 *exits the tavern ringing the tavern bell perfectly in time.* FANNY *spins around!*

Yes! The bell!

CLARA *looks over* FANNY*'s shoulder.*

CLARA. Yes! I think that works!

FANNY *is furiously scribbling.* LANDLADY *has reappeared.*

LANDLADY. Where's this money then?

MAN 1 *comes over to pay* LANDLADY.

MAN 1. Excuse me. Can I pay for our dinner?

LANDLADY. It's two marks and three pfennings.

FANNY. I'll pay your bill.

MAN 1. Oh hello, strangers.

LANDLADY. You want to pay *his* bill?

FANNY. Yes. How much was it?

LANDLADY. Two marks and three pfennings.

FANNY. Fine, that's nothing!

LANDLADY. Alright. Three marks and four pfennings then.

FANNY. What about double?!

LANDLADY. Four marks and five pfennings?!

FANNY. Perfect. Would you mind going away to get us something to drink?

LANDLADY. Fine. But then I want my money!

LANDLADY *exits.*

MAN 1. Thank you very much, sir.

MAN 1 *is about to exit.*

FANNY. Wait, wait, wait. I need something in return. Do you remember how you thumped that barrel?

MAN 1. Oh, you saw me thumping my barrel?

FANNY. A moment ago. I need you to thump that barrel again! Just exactly like you did!

MAN 1. I have to go and see my friend in the back of his carriage.

FANNY. I just paid for your dinner! Surely that can wait a moment? One moment, one, please, Bobby will teach you.

MAN 1. Oh, hello, Bobby.

CLARA. Hi.

FANNY. You'll do it?

MAN 1. Will Bobby teach me?

FANNY. Yeah, sure, Bobby, can you show him what to do?

FANNY *hands* CLARA *the score who begins teaching* MAN 1 *the timpani part.*

FANNY *looks around.*

Why is Wilhelm taking so long?! I need somebody to ring this bell!

FANNY *looks at the audience – she spots a woman in trousers.*

Ah, you. You'll do. Hello, fellow traveller, my name is Sebastian – yes, I am looking at you unfortunately. I'm a composer – gosh that feels amazing – I'm a *composer*! I need your help, would you mind helping me?

FANNY *vamps – importantly, doesn't ask her name – and brings the audience member up onstage.*

Fantastic – and you've already come disguised as a man! I'm not being rude – it's just 1830-something and you're wearing trousers! Have you ever played a musical instrument before? Is there any chance it was a doorbell? Well, it's very easy, when I point my baton at you, like this, you jangle the doorbell like this.

FANNY *demonstrates*.

Now you try! It's really easy, you can't get it wrong.

AUDIENCE *member tries*.

Oh, maybe you can get it wrong. Give it another go.

AUDIENCE *member tries again*.

Super. Now practise when I point the baton at you. The music will go... Bubbaduh bubbaduh bubbaduh bubbaduh – buh buh buh buh buh BUH! And then I'll point at you. Ready? Bubbaduh bubbaduh bubbaduh bubbaduh – buh buh buh buh buh BUH!

FANNY *points the baton and* AUDIENCE MEMBER *plays the bell*.

Well... it'll do. Bobby? Ready?

CLARA *pulls* FANNY *aside*.

CLARA. He says he wants me to go to the carriage with him and Dickie.

FANNY. You're a man now! Just say no. Right – same place. (*To* AUDIENCE MEMBER.) Are you ready?

MAN 1. Hang on! Bobby's an excellent teacher, thank you, Bobby, but I can't do both.

FANNY. What do you mean?

MAN 1. I've never played a musical instrument before and Bobby says I'm supposed to aurally represent a crescendoing timpani roll through an ascending vocal *glissando* as well as thump my barrel over four bars as if to conjure the rhythmic stabs of an entire orchestra!

FANNY. ...I see what you're saying. You concentrate on thumping your barrel.

FANNY turns to the audience and immediately addresses them as if they're her orchestra.

Ears on me, please.

She demonstrates the vocal glissando.

Yes. We'll try that please. (*Waving her baton to prepare them.*) I will give you two-three-breathe-sing. Yes? Like this. (*Demonstrates.*) Now you. And... two-three-breathe-sing!

She might repeat depending on the audience's ability.

Very good. Let's put it in context, Orchestra. DUM-pum-pum-pum-pum-pum-pum-pum diddlee-diddlee-diddlee-diddlee DUM-pum-pum-pum-pum-pum-pum-pum diddlee-diddlee-diddlee-diddlee. DUM-pum-pum-pum-pum-pum-pum-pum diddlee-TWO-THREE-BREATHE-SING!

The audience sings.

Wonderful. Thank you. Okay. Are we ready!

Music: 'Overture in C-major', Fanny Mendelssohn.

FANNY *conducts as:*

The audience sing, MAN 1 *thumps his barrel,* CLARA/FANNY *laugh and* AUDIENCE MEMBER *plays the bell.*

Okay! That works? I think that works! We need to talk about this bell though. How do you think that went? Yes. You bungled it, didn't you? Didn't you? Yes, you did.

CLARA. Sebastian...!

FANNY. Yes, what is it, Bobby?

CLARA. Can you please tell this fellow why I can't come to the carriage with him and Dickie?

LANDLADY slowly enters with a big tray of beer bottles.

FANNY. Listen, Bobby's had too much to drink, okay, his desire's there but his performance will not be. So, leave it.

MAN 1. He can watch.

FANNY. No he can't, Bobby and I are, we're like you and your friend, so – he can't.

MAN 1. The more the merrier!

FANNY. Look, we don't have... the right equipment.

MAN 1. We can order more butter!

LANDLADY *catches sight of the* AUDIENCE MEMBER *onstage.*

LANDLADY. Don't sit on that bench! Who is this?

FANNY *spins around* – CLARA *and* MAN 1 *continue talking,* sotto voce.

FANNY. This? This is, uh... well, yes... tell the Landlady your name.

AUDIENCE MEMBER *says their name.*

LANDLADY. A woman!

FANNY. No! No! That's not her name! (*Aside to* AUDIENCE MEMBER.) You're killing me here [audience name], no women are allowed in this tavern, remember! So your real name, your *male* first name is...

AUDIENCE MEMBER *makes up a name.*

FANNY. Really? You've gone with that? Okay, this is [made-up name]! Nobody here is a woman!

LANDLADY. Look, where's my money? You said that man was coming back with it, but I don't see him. You've got to pay for his dinner, your dinner, your rooms, these beers.

FANNY. I will pay.

LANDLADY. Now?

FANNY. In the fullness of time, when –

LANDLADY. You don't got no money, do you?

FANNY. I do, I really do, but the gentlemen who left, he was in charge of it and –

LANDLADY. Where is he?!

FANNY. What about a song?

LANDLADY. I'll tell you what I told Mozart: I'll take the money.

FANNY. I think you'll be surprised – I'm better than most are!

LANDLADY. Better than Mozart?

FANNY. No, better than most are. Look, Frau... Landlady, as someone with a clearly discerning respect for art, I wager you'd get far more joy and enrichment than mere money could ever bring you, by hearing a new orchestral work from a world-class composer!

LANDLADY. Who's that then?

FANNY. Me!

LANDLADY. I'll take the money.

FANNY. You haven't even heard it yet!

LANDLADY. I'll take the money.

FANNY. I refuse to let you insist on remuneration without even considering the worth of art. And don't even think about saying 'I'll take the money'! You will listen. Your mind will be opened. Give me that tray of drinks.

FANNY puts the tray of drinks down.

Stand down there. Bobby, give her the music.

LANDLADY positions herself downstage-centre in front of the imagined orchestra. CLARA puts the score in her hands.

FANNY drinks a little beer from each of the bottles.

LANDLADY. You've got to pay for that, you know!

FANNY. I know, I know but wait until you hear this! This is it, everyone! [Made-up name], don't mess this up. Right, here, look here.

FANNY *points to a bar in front of the* LANDLADY.

We're going from here. Ready?

FANNY *waves the orchestra in. As we are hearing this from the* LANDLADY*'s perspective there is silence.*

The audience sings, MAN 1 *thumps his barrel,* CLARA/ FANNY *laugh and* AUDIENCE MEMBER *plays the bell.*

Then FANNY *uses her baton to tap the bottles like a xylophone.*

Silence.

LANDLADY. I'll take the money.

FANNY. It was the doorbell wasn't it! Forget the doorbell! Go and sit down, [name], you've really made a mess of this!

AUDIENCE MEMBER *sits down.*

LANDLADY. I want my money!

CLARA. You're a philistine!

LANDLADY. I'm a businessman.

FANNY. It's okay, Clara, it's okay. Sit down, sit down.

FANNY *sits* CLARA *down on the sticky bench.*

I know exactly what we're going to do.

WILHELM *bursts into the tavern.*

Oh thank goodness because I really had nothing.

WILHELM. Fanny!

FANNY. Nope, no, no women here, *Eric*!

WILHELM. I mean Sebastian!

FANNY. I told you he'd come back.

MAN 1. Hello, Eric!

WILHELM. We have to go!

MAN 1. Have you ever spent the night in a carriage?

LANDLADY. Where's my money?!

FANNY. This man will now pay our bill.

FANNY sits down next to CLARA on the sticky bench.

LANDLADY. Come on then, gimme the money!

WILHELM. What money?

FANNY. You went to the carriage to get the money, Eric!

WILHELM. Oh yes. I didn't.

FANNY. What have you been doing?!

WILHELM. Exactly! We have to go!

LANDLADY. You're not going anywhere without paying! Where's my money?

WILHELM. I don't have it.

LANDLADY. You don't have it?

WILHELM. No.

LANDLADY. And *you* don't have it and *you* don't have it?

CLARA. No.

FANNY. Not at the moment, but –

LANDLADY. I'll tell you something. You know who else travels about without money?

FANNY. Who?

LANDLADY. Women!

FANNY. How many times – none of us are women!

As she finishes the line, she and CLARA *leap up emphatically – RIIIIIIIIIIIP!*

Their trousers, however, remain on the sticky bench, revealing their Victorian ladies' underwear.

LANDLADY *is shocked.*

Wait, wait, look, I can explain everything!

MAN 1. At last!

MAN 1 *tears off his own trousers to reveal Victorian ladies' underwear.*

FANNY. Nearly everything. I can explain nearly everything!

Suddenly the door to the tavern is kicked open and who should stroll in…? FELIX!

FELIX. Well, well, well… if it isn't my ambitious older sister.

FANNY. Felix!

MAN 1. Hello, Felix!

WILHELM. I tried to tell you!

MAN 1. Are you interested in learning to play the oboe?

FELIX. Whose pocket are you in now?!

FANNY. Brother, I can explain, I can…

FELIX. Oh, there'll be plenty of time to think of an explanation on your way back to Berlin.

FANNY. But, wait, hear me out first, brother –

CLARA *taps* FELIX *on the shoulder.*

FELIX. Not now, Clara.

CLARA. But, Felix…

FELIX. Not now!

CLARA. Kiss me, Felix! Kiss me!

FELIX.…What?!

FELIX *spins around and* CLARA *punches him right in the kisser.*

CLARA. RUN!!!!

FANNY, WILHELM *and* CLARA *flee the scene!*

As they exit they grab tablecloths/curtains to create makeshift skirts.

The Docks

FANNY, WILHELM *and* CLARA *run back to the docks at Hamburg.*

FANNY. We need to get to London, sir, with some immediacy!

BOATSWAIN. I'll tell you what I told you, ma'am, the same as previously,
There ain't no boats till morning, so go away, come back
And I'll get you on a boat just as soon as dawn has cracked.

FANNY. There must be something sooner!

BOATSWAIN. No, alas, no chips!
I've said, until the morning, that it's only cargo ships.

FANNY. We'll travel on a cargo boat – we really cannot wait!

BOATSWAIN. Well there's one with oil, one with clay and another one with paint.

FANNY. With paint? No! They all sound messy! We need to get to sea!

BOATSWAIN. There is one full of animals that's moored down at... dock three.

FANNY. We could travel with some animals, right?

CLARA. Yes, London isn't far.

BOATSWAIN. And now you come to mention it, it's leaving in a *trice*.

PART TWO   89

CLARA. That's perfect!

FANNY. Come on, let's go go go!

BOATSWAIN. Uh, no no no.
 I said: and now you come to mention it, it's leaving in a *trice*.

FANNY. What?

BOATSWAIN. In a trice…

CLARA. That's what we want!

BOATSWAIN. A trice. A *trice*!

FANNY. What's he talking about?

   BOATSWAIN *really emphasises the rhythm.*

BOATSWAIN. I said: And *now* you *come* to *men*tion *it*, it's *leav*ing *in* a *trice*.

WILHELM. Well come then, sir, I see your game, I bid you name your *price*.

BOATSWAIN. Who, *me*? You think *me*, a humble writer, might engage in vice!

   WILHELM *rummages about in his pockets.*

WILHELM. How would one mark sound? Or will you make us beg?

BOATSWAIN. One mark? Please! I'm not some low-cost…
 egg.

WILHELM. Two marks!

DOG. BARK BARK.

WILHELM. Three is all I've got!

BOATSWAIN. I'm sorry, mate,
 I'll tell you straight
 either pee or get off the pot.

WILHELM. More?

BOATSWAIN. Sure!
Plenty more!

WILHELM. Twenty more?

BOATSWAIN. You don't look poor!

WILHELM. My wallet, sir, is empty!

BOATSWAIN. So what?

WILHELM. I'll tell you what!
We're throwing in the towel!

BOATSWAIN. Your choice, sir, but I will say this, in the words of doggy:
Growl.

FANNY. Just tell us how much you want please, *matey*.

BOATSWAIN. Why don't we say, I think, seven and eighty?
Pounds.

FANNY. Pounds?! We've only got marks.

CLARA. I've got some francs.

WILHELM. What's francs to marks?

FANNY. How does that help?

WILHELM. I'll convert it and long-divide it over the square of the longest side.

CLARA. I don't understand.

WILHELM. Me neither...

FANNY. I never thought I'd say this but, I wish Paul were here.

BOATSWAIN. Tough, he's not!

FANNY. I tell you what, we'll, we'll pay you later!

BOATSWAIN. Later? Hmm. You'd need to give me proof.

That is, of course, if you want to –

DOG. WOOF WOOF WOOF!

BOATSWAIN. Sorry, my trusty pooch has no faith in you.

FANNY. The dog? And, what? That means?

BOATSWAIN. Remaining you.

FANNY. Sorry, what was that?

BOATSWAIN. Remaining you… You must remain.

DOG *whimpers*.

Shh!

FANNY. Well, we've got no more money!

BOATSWAIN. Oh, unless…

FANNY. What?

BOATSWAIN. You could show me what's beneath your dress. Instead.

FANNY. What?!

BOATSWAIN. You heard exactly what I said.

FANNY. And what exactly are you hoping to see beneath my dress?

WILHELM. Fanny!

BOATSWAIN. Well…

FANNY. If I show you my ankle, will you let us board the boat?

CLARA. Don't do it.

BOATSWAIN. Thigh.

FANNY. Calf.

BOATSWAIN. Knee.

FANNY. Deal.

WILHELM. Fanny…

FANNY. I know, Wilhelm, I know, but sometimes you do something you know to be wrong to get something you know to be right.

WILHELM covers his eyes with his hands.

What are you doing?

WILHELM. I'll see them when you want to show them to me.

FANNY. That's very sweet, Wilhelm, but you did just see them in the tavern a moment ago.

FANNY flashes BOATSWAIN her knees. His mouth is suddenly very dry.

BOATSWAIN. Dock three. Tell Aitor I said you could stow away in the hold.

FANNY. Come on – this way!

FANNY, CLARA and WILHELM exit towards dock three.

BOATSWAIN. The sight of hinged knees
To me will never wither
Even as the Knobbly Princess
Runs off, fleeing, thither.

The DOG whines/whimpers in a disapproving way.
BOATSWAIN sighs heavily.

Maybe I'm bad at this.

FANNY runs back on.

FANNY. You know, not all poems have to rhyme.

She exits. A light bulb goes off in BOATSWAIN's head.

BOATSWAIN begins singing a surprisingly beautiful rhymeless sea shanty.

BOATSWAIN.
Sail on, sail on, mate,
Just keep on, sailing on
Might be the mist on the water
Might be the sun in your eye
But it might be what you're after
So keep on sailing on.

They'll tie you to the harbour
If you don't keep sailing on.
(etc.)

Through some kind of theatre trickery, FANNY*'s boat sails across the Channel towards England.*

The Boat

The sea shanty continues – perhaps hummed under the scene. Storm sounds – thunder and lightning.

Inside the hold on the boat – FANNY *is scribbling on her manuscript.*

FANNY *grabs her baton and waves in the orchestra. (Flute solo, bar 230.)*

It's not right. She scribbles again. Waves orchestra in again.

It's still not right. She scribbles again. Waves in the orchestra again.

It's worse.

CLARA *steps into the room.* FANNY *stops writing and gives* CLARA *a smile.*

FANNY. Much less animal faeces.

CLARA. What?

FANNY. When I dreamt about this moment, there was much less animal faeces.

CLARA. ...but there was still *some*?

FANNY. Oh, even in my wildest dreams I can't escape the fact that Wagner's still alive.

CLARA. You know what's wonderful about Wagner?

FANNY. No.

CLARA. Me neither!

> FANNY *enjoys the joke*. CLARA *hovers at the door.*
>
> Wilhelm is feeling better.

FANNY. That's good.

> CLARA *edges into the room.*

CLARA. Still going?

FANNY. I can't capture it.

CLARA. Sometimes it's *larghissimo*, you know?

FANNY. I'm struggling with a flute solo.

CLARA. Oh, maybe you're seasick, too?

FANNY. I've got plenty of notes, but I haven't got that...

CLARA. ...inevitable thing?

FANNY. Exactly. I think what I'm writing sounds as phoney as the journey we're on.

> CLARA *comes and sits down next to* FANNY.

CLARA. Do you know why I came to Berlin?

FANNY. Was it to share a berth with a couple of chickens and a goat?

CLARA. I came to give Felix something. This. Here.

> CLARA *offers some manuscript papers.*

FANNY. What is it?

CLARA. A concerto. Mine.

> FANNY *looks at* CLARA*'s outstretched hands.*
>
> I want to offer it to you.

FANNY. Oh... why?

CLARA. If you'd like it.

FANNY. What for?

CLARA. Well, we'll be in London soon –

FANNY. And?

CLARA. If you feel there's a gap in the programme –

FANNY. You mean if my work is not ready?

CLARA. No, I just thought it might take the pressure off –

FANNY. To know you're waiting in the wings?

CLARA. To know there's an alternative.

FANNY *takes this in*.

FANNY. Something will come.

CLARA. I don't doubt it.

FANNY. I think you do doubt it.

CLARA. Not at all.

FANNY. It's just process.

CLARA. It wouldn't have to be instead of yours – we could replace the Bach.

FANNY. And compete against each other?

CLARA. I thought of it quite differently.

FANNY. I'm sure you did.

CLARA. Have I upset you?

FANNY. Upset? I'm not the slightest bit upset.

CLARA. Okay.

FANNY. Okay.

CLARA. Because it's just an offer.

FANNY. Okay.

CLARA. It is.

CLARA *is silent*.

FANNY. Was there something else?

There's a moment.

CLARA. Even if we can't play it, I'd like to hear your thoughts.

FANNY. It needs work.

CLARA. You haven't looked at it!

FANNY. You think it's perfect?

CLARA. No.

FANNY. Then it needs work.

CLARA. Maybe I've overstepped but –

FANNY. I have to get back to this flute.

CLARA. I'm showing you an open wound!

FANNY. Would you keep an eye on Wilhelm for me?

CLARA. Fanny – ?

FANNY. Here – find a needle and thread and sew it up yourself.

FANNY chucks the score towards CLARA. It lands on the floor. CLARA doesn't pick it up.

He's up on deck, I think.

CLARA walks to the exit and stops.

What?

CLARA. I'm very much looking forward to the concert, Frauline Mendelssohn.

CLARA exits. FANNY watches her go and then leaps up and grabs CLARA's manuscript.

She brings the orchestra in.

Music: Piano Concerto in A-minor, Op. 7: *'Finale: Allegro non troppo – Allegro molto'*, Clara Schumann.

(*Suggested extract: opening to bar 35.*)

Initially FANNY *isn't overly impressed. She's a little surprised when the orchestra joins in bars 13/14.*

As the horns come in in bar 19 and the strings in 20, FANNY *begins to look worried.*

This quickly turns to awe in bar 24. Astonishment and fear builds through bars 31–35.

FANNY *pulls the music tight to her chest. Silence.*

She looks around as if to check if anyone else has heard what she has.

She whips the manuscript open again and flicks through a little further:

Music: Piano Concerto in A-minor, Op. 7: *'Finale: Allegro non troppo – Allegro molto', Clara Schumann.*

FANNY *flicks through further:*

Music: Piano Concerto in A-minor, Op. 7: *'Finale: Allegro non troppo – Allegro molto', Clara Schumann.*

FANNY *flicks through further:*

Music: Piano Concerto in A-minor, Op. 7: *'Finale: Allegro non troppo – Allegro molto', Clara Schumann.*

The final notes echo and reverb around FANNY.

FANNY *stumbles as if the boat has just hit something.*

VOICE (*off*). WEST INDIA DOCKS! THAT'S WEST INDIA DOCKS! THAT'S LONDON, PEOPLE!

FANNY *stands still, shocked, centre-stage.*

A carriage appears around her…

The Carriages

CLARA *takes her manuscript from* FANNY. WILHELM *puts* FANNY*'s sheet music into her hands.*

FANNY *seems almost not to notice. She sits – trance-like.*

WILHELM. Oh look, the Tower of London!

FANNY. What…?

WILHELM. It's the Tower – look, look. I'm going to sketch it!

FANNY *doesn't look – she turns to* WILHELM *who starts sketching.*

FANNY. We're nearly there?

WILHELM. I think so! Clara?

CLARA (*to the* DRIVER). How long will it take to the Royal Palace, sir?

DRIVER. Tricky t'say, depends if we hit traffic round St Paul's.

FANNY. Roughly?

DRIVER (*does a rough voice*). Tricky t'say, depends if we – (*Goes back to normal.*) Nah, I'm only messing with you. An hour? Give or take.

CLARA. That long?

DRIVER. Sorry, we're going top speed!

WILHELM. What's that?

DRIVER. Two horsepower.

CLARA. And you can't go any quicker?

DRIVER. I'd have to get another horse!

FANNY. Can you go any slower?

DRIVER. You want me to go slower?

FANNY. Could we walk from here?

PART TWO 99

DRIVER. Walk! You want to walk along the north bank?!

FANNY. No, I suppose not.

CLARA. Fanny, let me take a look?

FANNY. What? No.

FANNY hides her sheet music from CLARA.

I don't need your help.

Suddenly the carriage lurches to the right! WILHELM *draws an erroneous line on his sketch.*

WILHELM. Damn it!

FANNY. Driver, what was that?

WILHELM. It's fine! I'll make it into a tree.

It lurches to the right again!

FANNY. Driver?

DRIVER. Dunno, pal!

It lurches to the right again!

WILHELM. Argh! I guess that's two trees!

FANNY. Driver?

DRIVER. Some madman keeps ramming his carriage into us.

FELIX *pops his head through the carriage window – he is spattered with paint.*

FELIX. Hello, sister!

FANNY. Brother?!

CLARA. You crossed the North Sea?!

LEA *sticks her head in through the carriage window – she is covered in paint.*

CLARA. Oh, you got *that* boat.

LEA. Fanny! Are you safe?

FANNY. Mother, your dress!

FELIX. That invitation was meant for me, Fanny!

CLARA. Because you told the Queen you'd written 'Italien'!

FELIX. Who told you that?!

FANNY. What do you mean?

CLARA. Wait, who's driving your carriage?

> LEA *and* FELIX *look at each other and then hurl themselves back into the other carriage.*
>
> FANNY *runs to the carriage window.*

FANNY. Wait! Come back! What did you say about the Queen?

CLARA. Driver, I need you to get us to the Royal Palace as quickly as you can!

FANNY. Wait a moment, driver –

CLARA. Ignore him, Fanny. Do you think we'll make it without stopping?

DRIVER. 'Pends if I gotta fill her up.

CLARA. Fill who up?

DRIVER. Her or her.

FANNY. Who?

DRIVER. The horses.

WILHELM. What do you fill up horses with?

DRIVER. 'Ay.

WILHELM. I said, 'What do you fill up horses with?'

DRIVER. Yeah, 'n' I said wiv hay. Hay for the horses.

> *The carriage swerves to the right – another erroneous line for* WILHELM*'s sketch.*

WILHELM. GAH! It's fine, fine!

FANNY. Felix said –

They get hit again, swerving right!

WILHELM. Again?!

CLARA. What's going on?!

They get hit again, swerving right!

WILHELM. It's not London – I'm sketching a forest!

FANNY. What did Felix mean, Clara?

CLARA. Driver, gee them up!

FANNY. Wait! Clara –

CLARA. We can talk about it later but now we need to go!

FANNY. But –

CLARA. Driver, pull away from them!

DRIVER. I'm trying!

They get hit again, swerving right!

WILHELM. Whoa!

FANNY. What did he mean about '*Italien*'?

CLARA. *Presto presto*! We've got twice the horsepower!

DRIVER. I know!

FANNY. Clara –

CLARA. He's lying to you!

FANNY. I don't think he was.

They get hit again, swerving right!

WILHELM. Whoa! Whoa!

FANNY. I need to talk to him.

CLARA. Why are the horses slowing down?!

DRIVER. 'Cos he keeps shouting 'whoa'!

FANNY. Whoa?

They get hit again, swerving right!

WILHELM. Whoa! Whoa! Whoa!

DRIVER. Yeah! He's speaking horse!

They get hit again, swerving right!

WILHELM. Whoa!

FANNY. *Whoa*, Wilhelm, you've got to stop saying *whoa*, yes *WHOA*, stop saying *WHOA! WHOA!*

DRIVER. Tell them both to shut it.

CLARA. Just ram them back!

DRIVER. Alright! Here we gooooo!

Right at the moment of impact we cut to the Mendelssohn carriage! FELIX *is driving the horses.*

FELIX. Damn it, they're pulling away from us! Faster! Faster!

LEA. I think we're at top speed!

FELIX. We need another horse!

LEA. Maybe we should just allow her a moment?

FELIX. You mean give her what she wants?!

LEA. Or maybe could you let her publish?

FELIX. I've published her under my name! As if it were mine!

LEA. There must be something!

FELIX. I know what I need to do. Take the reins and ram them!

LEA. What?

FELIX. Just do it! Ram them again!

LEA. Okay... Here we gooooo!

Right at the moment of impact we cut to FANNY*'s carriage! The carriage swerves to the right.*

WILHELM. Whoaa –

    CLARA *pounces on him.*

CLARA. Stop saying that word!

    FELIX *pops his head into the carriage window.*

FELIX. Pull over, Fanny! Let's talk!

FANNY. Yes! I want to talk!

CLARA. Never!

FELIX. I want to apologise to you, very truthfully.

FANNY. Brother, the Queen –

FELIX. I'm sincerely, honestly sorry that I didn't listen to you –

FANNY. Brother –

FELIX. That I couldn't hear what you were saying to me.

FANNY. Brother!

FELIX. Don't interrupt me when I'm apologising to you! I'm sorry that I didn't tell *you* about the Queen. I'm sorry! But did I tell *her* about *you*!

FANNY. What?

FELIX. I told her '*Italien*' was written by my sister –

FANNY. What…?

FELIX. By YOU! And she still invited *me*!

CLARA. He's lying!

FANNY. You're lying!

CLARA. She's earned this place!

FELIX. Has she? Have you earned this, Fanny?

CLARA. Felix! Felix!

FELIX. Going to pretend to kiss me, Clara?

CLARA. Nope.

CLARA grabs a cricket bat – she swings to whack FELIX but she bashes WILHELM in the nose.

His nose starts bleeding.

I'm sorry!

FANNY. Wilhelm, are you okay?

FANNY runs to WILHELM to see if he's okay.

CLARA continues her swing and whacks FELIX – sending him tumbling back into his own carriage.

Right as he's hit we cut back to the Mendelssohn carriage.

FELIX. They hit me with a cricket bat!

LEA. Could you see Fanny? Was she okay?

FELIX. Mother! They hit me with a cricket bat!

LEA. The pompousness! What's wrong with a fist? Get back in there!

FELIX. No.

LEA. Pull yourself together and get back into that carriage!

FELIX. I don't want to.

LEA. You'll be fine.

FELIX. You do it then!

LEA. Would your father let a cricket bat stop him?

FELIX. Fanny's practically on top of Herr Hensel!

LEA. No she isn't!

FELIX. She is! She's all over him.

LEA. Here! Hold these! I'm going in!

LEA hands the reins over.

LEA. Ram them again!

SLAM! FANNY's carriage! The carriage swerves to the right.

FANNY pushes WILHELM's head out of the far window, his nose to the sky.

He is desperately clutching it and whimpering.

FANNY. That's it! That's it!

FANNY steps between WILHELM's legs and puts one hand under his back to hold him up.

CLARA *kneels behind* FANNY. *The carriage is bumpy.*

Yes, that's it, yes, that's it, you'll be okay, I know what I'm doing.

LEA pops her head in through the carriage window and sees a totally different version of events.

She slowly retreats back into her own carriage.

The Mendelssohn carriage. LEA *sits down at the back of the carriage in total shock.*

FELIX. What's the matter?

LEA *waves him off and shakes her head – she might be about to throw up.*

What is it?

LEA. I think we might need to send for a bishop.

FELIX. What?! I'm going to ram them again!

LEA. Alright...

FELIX. Here we go!

SLAM! We see the two carriages racing alongside one another! They shout between them.

Fanny!

LEA. Pull over! Pull over, Fanny! Come home!

CLARA. Faster driver! FASTER!

FELIX. It was cruel to say that marriage was the end for us. It needn't be.

FANNY. What do you mean?

FELIX. Wilhelm was right!

WILHELM. I was?

CLARA. *Presto!*

LEA. Slow down!

FELIX. We both know you don't want to do this!

LEA. Think of us!

FELIX. You don't want to bring shame onto the family.

LEA. For once in your life –

FELIX. You just want to be heard.

LEA. – think of us!

FELIX. And I hear you, Fanny! I hear you!

FANNY. You do?

FELIX. You want to be published?

CLARA. Driver! *Prestissimo!*

FANNY. To be published?

FELIX. I will arrange for your orchestral work to be published.

CLARA. Come on! Prrrrrruh-puhpuhpuhpuhpuh!

FANNY. Wait, but –

FELIX. Under your name! We'll publish under your name!

CLARA. Don't trust him!

FELIX. Let me see it!

FANNY. It's my only copy!

FELIX. I need to see it.

FANNY. I, I ...

CLARA. Don't!

FELIX. Hand it over.

> FELIX *leans across and swipes* FANNY*'s sheet music from her.*

Gosh, it's your finest work, truly... Oops!

> FELIX *flings* FANNY*'s sheet music out of the carriage and into the street!*

FANNY. No!

> FANNY *runs to the window and watches it flutter into the distance.*

FELIX. See how far ingratitude gets you!

CLARA. *Accelerando! Vivacissimo!*

DRIVER. Go on, horses!

> *The Mendelssohn carriage starts pulling away.*

CLARA. That's it!

FELIX. Go as quick as you like! You've got nothing! See you at the palace!

> FELIX *disappears into his own carriage.*

CLARA. It's fine! Keep going!

> *The Mendelssohn carriage is out of sight.*

FANNY. Stop the carriage.

CLARA. Faster, driver, faster!

FANNY. Stop the carriage!

CLARA. Fanny, it's okay – we can –

FANNY. Get him to stop. Stop!

WILHELM. Will you stop please, driver.

DRIVER. Eh?

CLARA. Keep going, driver.

FANNY. Wilhelm, make him stop!

WILHELM. Stop!

CLARA. Keep going, driver!

WILHELM. Stop the horses! Stop the horses! Stop! Stop the horses!

FANNY. Stop! STOP!

CLARA. Fanny!

FANNY. STOP THE CARRIAGE!

She means it this time. FANNY *leans forwards and grabs the reins from* DRIVER.

WHOAAAAA!!!!!!

London Streets

The carriage disappears. FANNY *is almost hyperventilating.*

WILHELM. Fanny?

FANNY. I'm making the worst mistake.

CLARA. Fanny – ?

FANNY. We're not playing it, Clara! Okay?!

WILHELM. Fanny –

FANNY. Why did I think I had any right to bend my life? I could sit at home and be quiet and have babies and be happy! I could be happy because it's a nice life – it's a nice life, Wilhelm! I've got a nice life and I should be happy with it!

WILHELM. Fanny –

FANNY. I mean, Jesus, Clara, and her father,[34] and Robert, and she's got children! And yet here she is because – I'm right, aren't I, Clara? – you've travelled halfway across Europe, even when I've been vile to you, because you need money! Right? Not recognition, Wilhem – money: for food and shoes and doctors!

CLARA. Calm, Fanny –

FANNY. I AM CALM! And I can't even write a piece of music for an opportunity I've stolen! Felix is right! I'm not a serious musician! I'm a farce! This isn't a dream! It's a nightmare! I'm living in a nightmare!

FANNY suddenly stops – there's terror in her eyes – something is seriously wrong.

Wilhelm…?

WILHELM. What is it?

FANNY. I can't feel my hands.[35]

A strange stillness descends. Nobody knows what to do.

Wilhelm?

FELIX runs onto the stage.

FELIX. Well, well, well, at last –

FELIX senses something is wrong.

What's the matter?

FANNY. I can't feel my hands.

FELIX looks at FANNY as if to confirm what she's said. There's a moment between them.

FELIX. Wilhelm, we need a bowl of warm vinegar.

WILHELM. Where do –

FELIX. You'll find it. You're okay, look at me, you're going to be okay. As quick as you can, please, Wilhelm.

WILHELM exits.

This way, that's it, you're okay, you're going to sit down here for a moment next to your horrible younger brother.

FELIX guides FANNY onto a bench.

CLARA. Felix?

FELIX. I need you to fetch Mother.

CLARA *exits*.

Steady breaths.

FANNY. It's like Father!

FELIX. No it isn't. You haven't spent your life eating butter and sugar. Keep breathing – I might not be a physician but I do know breathing is very important. Am I breathing?

FANNY. Yes.

FELIX. That's how important it is. As long as I'm here nothing can hurt you, Fanny. Just breathe. Slowly. That's it.

FELIX *gestures to his sister's hands*.

Can I?

FANNY *nods*. FELIX *kneels in front of* FANNY *and picks up her hands. He looks at her – can she feel it?*

FANNY *shakes her head – she's scared*.

That's very normal – the papers always compliment my delicate touch.

He starts massaging them. He's very calm. After a moment...

How's your brain? That's still working, isn't it?

FANNY *nods*.

Good, what do you think of this melody?

He starts humming.

Humming: Lieder ohne Worte, *'Op. 38: No. 2. Allegro non troppo in C-minor, "Lost Happiness"'*.

FANNY. Felix –

FELIX. Wait, it gets good, I promise –

He keeps humming and massaging. This continues until the mood calms.

After a few moments, FANNY *gives him a look.*

What?

There's a glint in FANNY's *eye.* FELIX *knows what's coming.*

What?

FANNY. After the A-flat I'd have gone F-sharp G rather than G F-sharp.

FELIX *hums both versions.*

FELIX. Very good. How are they?

FANNY. Better.

FELIX. They've come back to life?

FANNY. Yes.

FELIX. I knew they would. My hands! A gift from God.

FELIX *sits down on the bench next to* FANNY.

FANNY. Thank you.

FELIX. Oh, please. As with everything in my life, it was an entirely selfish act: I don't know what I'd do without you.

FANNY. I don't know what you'd do either.

FELIX. Monster. I'm sorry, Fanny.

FANNY. What for?

FELIX *thinks for a moment.*

FELIX. I suppose I'm sorry that you're my sister.

FANNY *takes this in.*

FANNY. Will you take Clara with you?

FELIX. What if she hits me?

FANNY. Sometimes you deserve it.

FANNY *hands* FELIX *a manuscript.*

You must premiere her work.

FELIX. I'll read it.

FANNY. It's unfettered, it's a force, Felix. You must premiere it. That's my condition.

FELIX. You are in no position to bargain.

FANNY....!

FELIX *takes the manuscript*.

FELIX. But I trust you.

CLARA *and* LEA *enter*.

LEA. Fanny!

FANNY. I'm okay.

LEA. Come here, give me your hands!

FANNY. It's a false alarm. I'm fine.

LEA. Let me hold them!

FANNY *does so* – LEA *feels them*.

You can feel this?

FANNY. I'm okay, honestly.

LEA. You're sure?

FANNY. I'm sure.

LEA. Well... good. I'm pleased.

FANNY. Are you?

LEA. No! I'm so cross! How could you be so stupid?! You've dragged us across Europe, we've risked our lives in a carriage chase, and now... now you've scared us, I thought...! And look at me – I'm the human embodiment of a painter's smock!

FANNY. Will you take me home?

LEA. No, let's go to the bloody zoo![36] Of course we're going home!

FELIX. I must leave you, now.

FANNY. Good luck, brother.

FELIX. Clara?

CLARA. Yes?

FELIX. Would you do me the honour of joining me at the Royal Palace?

CLARA. You want me to play?

FELIX. I think, perhaps, we should play this.

CLARA. Fanny – ?

FANNY. Nothing to do with me.

FELIX. I'm going to my lodgings to change. What say you?

CLARA. Yes.

FELIX. Wonderful.

CLARA. But I'm not coming to your lodgings.

FELIX. Understood. We'll meet at the palace but we must be quick! Take my carriage. This way.

FELIX exits with CLARA.

FANNY exhales for what feels like the first time.

FANNY. I'm sorry, Mother.

LEA. Oh, don't...

FANNY. I am.

LEA. Stop it.

LEA can see how upset FANNY is. She decides to sit down next to her.

I like that you're ambitious. I'm not sure I've ever said that.

The compliment isn't enough.

I was ambitious once too, you know.

FANNY. You were?

LEA *holds her daughter's gaze.*

What happened?

LEA. I have you.

FANNY *thinks.*

FANNY. Are you happy, Mother?

LEA. I have you.

FANNY. Oh God, I hope that means yes.

LEA. Of course it means yes! Shall I tell you the worst of married life?

FANNY. What?

LEA. Once the ring is on his finger a lack of restraint will appear when it comes to breaking wind.

FANNY. That doesn't seem so bad.

LEA. Well… sometimes it seems worse than others.

FANNY *smiles.*

Are you very sad?

FANNY. Stupid.

LEA. You're not stupid for wanting things to change, Fanny – it's just that we have to play the music that gets handed to us.

FANNY. Will it be different for my daughter?

LEA *can't answer the question.*

Well… when?

The truth isn't what either of them want to hear. FANNY *is disheartened.*

LEA. My very first instinct when you were born was to look at your hands.[37] You had the most delicate little fingers. You'll think I'm mad but as soon as I saw them, I knew. I just knew,

Fanny, I could feel it. I knew what you were capable of. And in that moment I promised myself that I was going to give you everything – everything that I could – and when Felix came along of course what he had was different, as it must be, but I made sure you didn't fall behind. And you didn't! Of course you didn't! You led the way! But, you're not a child any more, you're a woman, and I feel as if I set you up to fall. I promised you something that deep down I knew you could never have. But the truth is that every time I looked at you, all I could see was my beautiful baby with the delicate fingers – and, I know it must seem cruel now, but I just didn't want you to waste it.

FANNY *takes a long preparatory inbreath.*

FANNY. Oh God.

FANNY *stands up.*

I have to go.

LEA. Where?

FANNY. We don't *just* play what gets handed to us – we contribute. We're in the middle of this stave that runs the length of history and we just have to add whatever notes we can, as best we can, and hope that somewhere up ahead those notes we've added will help push the music on.

LEA. What are you going to do?

FANNY. Maybe I'll hoik my skirts up and take a crap on the piano.

LEA. Fanny!

FANNY. I think it's okay to do something you know to be wrong to get something that you know to be right.

LEA. Oh God, are you actually going to crap on a piano…?

WILHELM *comes onto stage – he's holding some very muddy papers.*

WILHELM. You're standing up.

FANNY. I am.

WILHELM. You're okay?

FANNY. I'm fine.

> WILHELM *goes to* FANNY *and holds her as though he'll never let her go.*

LEA. Some men never change. Herr Hensel! Please!

FANNY. Wilhelm, my love –

> WILHELM *lets go of* FANNY.

LEA. This is a public place!

FANNY. Where have you been?

WILHELM. I couldn't find any warm vinegar, and my English isn't so good, and then I thought that maybe if I couldn't find it that you might – because you really didn't seem very well – and I thought it might be my fault, and then I thought that to me your work is like medicine so maybe it would be medicine to you, so then I ran back to Eastcheap –

FANNY. You ran to Eastcheap?

WILHELM. And back. And I picked up this. I think I have almost all of it.

FANNY. My orchestral work.

WILHELM. I'm sorry it's so muddy.

FANNY. Thank you, Wilhelm.

WILHELM. I'd just like to say out loud, I'm so happy you're not dead.

FANNY. Me too. Wilhelm, you gotta do something for me. Two things actually.

WILHELM. Anything.

FANNY. You won't enjoy it, but I need you to go to Felix's lodgings and kick him. Hard.

WILHELM. What!

FANNY. And if he gets up, kick him again. Then snap his baton in half and get the doctor over to cover him in leeches. Do everything you can to make sure that Felix does not leave his lodgings tonight.

WILHELM. Done. What else?

FANNY. Take off all your clothes.

LEA. Fanny!

WILHELM. When?

FANNY. At your earliest convenience, Herr Hensel!

WILHELM *starts undressing very quickly.*

LEA. Fanny –

FANNY. Don't worry, Mother. You get to listen now. These next few bars are mine.

LEA. What are you going to do?

FANNY *smiles.* WILHELM *hands* FANNY *his clothes.*

FANNY. Thank you, Wilhelm. Right!

FANNY *is about to start running.*

WILHELM. Wait! I don't actually have to kick him, do I?

FANNY *smiles.*

FANNY. Maybe just a little one…

FANNY *starts running.*

FANNY *stays centre-stage. She runs and runs across London towards the concert hall!*

As she runs, the rest of the cast help her to dress herself in the image of FELIX *using* WILHELM*'s clothes.*

Music swells.

Backstage at the Royal Palace

A STAGEHAND *is talking to a* STAGE BOY.

STAGEHAND. One job! One job – get Felix Mendelssohn, she said!

STAGE BOY. He'll be here, sir, I've got a feeling.

STAGEHAND. Well let's all relax then! Relax everyone because Herb here has got a feeling!

STAGE BOY. I could dance, sir, I'm good at dancing!

STAGEHAND. How many times – you're not dancing for the queen! Ah, I'm panicking!

STAGE BOY. Don't panic, sir, there's still time.

MAESTRO *enters*.

MAESTRO. Time's up! Where is he?!

STAGEHAND. He'll be here any moment, sir. Herb's got a feeling. Haven't you, Herb?

STAGE BOY. Oh yes.

MAESTRO. You've got about five minutes until the Queen is seated. Then your head is on the block!

STAGEHAND. Very funny, sir! Very funny!

STAGEHAND *laughs eccentrically*. MAESTRO *exits*.

Oh god… I wish I could just click my fingers and he'd be here!

STAGE BOY. Have you tried that, sir?

STAGEHAND. Have I tried clicking my fingers to see if I can magic up Felix Mendelssohn?!

STAGE BOY. Worth a go, sir…?

STAGEHAND. Alright, Herb, here you go, look at me clicking. I summon Felix Mendelssohn!

STAGEHAND *clicks his fingers.* FANNY (*dressed as* FELIX) *launches onto stage.*

FANNY. I'm here, Felix Mendelssohn!

STAGEHAND *spins around excitedly!*

STAGEHAND. What?!

FANNY. Sorry, I'm late.

STAGEHAND. Oh God.

FANNY. Who do I talk to about getting these to the orchestra?

STAGEHAND. What's this! Herb, what's this?

FANNY. I'm Felix Mendelssohn.

STAGE BOY. It's Felix Mendelssohn, sir.

STAGEHAND. No it's not! I know Felix Mendelssohn! I know him! Herb, I know him! Get away! Get away from here!

STAGEHAND *starts clicking at* FANNY.

FANNY. What are you doing?

STAGEHAND. How do I get rid of it, Herb?

STAGE BOY. I don't know, sir.

FANNY. Which way to the stage?

STAGEHAND. Shut up! Oh, and another thing, shut up! What do we do, Herb? I know, I know! Yes! Herb, go and get that sarcastic parrot!

STAGE BOY. I could dance, sir?

STAGEHAND. Do you promise you're a good dancer?

STAGE BOY *dances.*

STAGEHAND. Fine! You put your dancing shoes on and I'll deal with the Mendelssohn impersonator. Go. GO!

STAGE BOY *runs off –* MAESTRO *enters.*

MAESTRO. Three minutes!

STAGEHAND. Here he is, sir. Felix Mendelssohn!

FANNY. Here I am!

STAGEHAND. Stay over there. Told you he'd be here! Don't look at him, sir, he doesn't like to be looked at! Back you go, sir, quick as you can back behind the curtain, that's it, off you go.

MAESTRO. Three minutes!

STAGEHAND. Very good, sir, you're too generous, sir, thank you, sir, thank you.

STAGEHAND *bundles* MAESTRO *offstage*.

What am I going to do?!

FANNY. If only there was a Felix Mendelssohn here, ready to play.

STAGEHAND. I'm going to die.

FANNY. Get Clara Schumann. She'll tell you. She'll tell you that I'm Felix Mendelssohn.

STAGEHAND. I'm afraid that Clara Schumann has asked specifically not to see you, sir.

FANNY. Tell her that Fanny Mendelssohn would like to talk to her.

STAGEHAND. Fanny Mendelssohn?!

FANNY. My sister.

STAGEHAND. That's all I need! I'm not wearing a clean neckerchief! And I didn't brush my shoes. Or my hair. Or my teeth.

FANNY. You'd like to meet my sister?

STAGEHAND. Stop calling her your sister!

FANNY. Do you know her?

STAGEHAND. Have you heard her music – I adore her.

FANNY. Have *you*?

STAGEHAND. Sometimes when I'm tidying up your things, *his* things, *Felix's* things, my eyes have fallen across the music she's sent you, *him*. She's more dissonant than he is – she seems to plumb emotions in a way that he, and I mean no offence by this, can't.

FELIX *enters – maybe he's limping.*

FELIX. Prepare the orchestra at once!

STAGEHAND. Of course. I cannot tell you how happy I am to see you! I feel like I might jump with joy! I might actually jump! Would you mind if I jumped?

FELIX. If you must.

STAGEHAND *jumps.*

STAGEHAND. Bit strange actually, wasn't it. Let's get the inimitable Felix Mendelssohn to the stage.

FANNY. Absolutely, Bernard – let's go!

STAGEHAND. This is Felix Mendelssohn.

FANNY. No, I'm Felix Mendelssohn!

FELIX. No, I'm Felix Mendelssohn!

CLARA *enters.*

CLARA. Felix?

FELIX *and* FANNY (*together*). Yes.

CLARA. What's going on?

FANNY. I'm Felix Mendelssohn –

FELIX. No you're not!

FELIX *and* FANNY (*together*). I'm Felix Mendelssohn. No, I am. I am. I am!

FANNY. Clara! Clara, look at me, you recognise me, don't you, Clara?

FELIX. Argh! Give it up, Fanny! This is the other Mendelssohn!

STAGEHAND. You're Fanny Mendelssohn?

MAESTRO *enters*.

MAESTRO. What's going on?!

STAGEHAND (*of* FANNY). This is Felix Mendelssohn!

FELIX. What…

MAESTRO. I know! You said! Who the heck is this?!

STAGEHAND. He's an imposter! Turning up to the Royal Palace to steal the great F. Mendelssohn's moment!

MAESTRO. Get rid of him!

STAGEHAND. Of course.

MAESTRO. This way, sir.

FELIX. Wait! I order you to wait! Have you all lost your minds?! Clara, talk some sense into them! Tell them the truth – tell them that I'm Felix Mendelssohn.

CLARA *doesn't know what to do*.

Clara! Come on! How long have I known you?! I've taught you, introduced you, let you premiere my work! I've lifted you up, Clara, I've supported you! Tell them the truth. Return the favour.

FANNY. I've also let you down, though, Clara, haven't I? I have – *me*. I've given you far less than you deserve and I'm not asking you to forgive me but I do want you to know that I will do better next time.

CLARA. I've known Felix Mendelssohn since I was sixteen. He has been very kind to me. But whoever conducts tonight, the history of Felix Mendelssohn will be fine. (*Of* FANNY.) This is Felix Mendelssohn.

FELIX. WHAT?!

STAGE BOY. I knew it!

FELIX. I'm Felix Mendelssohn! I'm Felix Mendelssohn!

FANNY. You know, the more you say it the less believable it sounds.

FELIX. Get out my way!

STAGEHAND. Call the Queen's Guard!

FELIX. I'M FELIX MENDELSSOHN!

FANNY. Come here! Now!

> FANNY *pulls* FELIX *away from the group.*

> You know that I wouldn't ever hurt you.

> FELIX *is quiet.*

> They've come to see me, Felix. Everyone in this theatre is here for me. Not you.

> FELIX *is quiet.*

> They want to hear me.

> FELIX *seems to look out at the audience. Does he understand? He climbs from the stage and exits through front-of-house.*

MAESTRO. At last! We've got less than a minute!

> STAGE BOY *enters in a tutu.*

STAGE BOY. I'm ready! I'm ready to dance!

MAESTRO. What's this?

STAGE BOY. You said I could dance, didn't you sir?

STAGEHAND. Don't be ridiculous!

STAGE BOY. But –

STAGEHAND. Herb, you look like a slug digesting and umbrella. Go.

STAGE BOY. But –

STAGEHAND. Go!

> STAGE BOY *exits.*

MAESTRO. Come on! This way!

STAGEHAND. Wait! He needs a moment, sir, just a moment, to gather himself.

MAESTRO. Seconds! You've got seconds!

MAESTRO *exits*.

STAGEHAND. You're really Fanny Mendelssohn?

FANNY. I am.

STAGEHAND. It's an honour to meet you. Allow me to introduce myself.

STAGEHAND *pulls a clip out of her hair and reveals herself to also be in disguise.*

FANNY *and* CLARA *are shocked.*

FANNY. Bernard!

STAGEHAND. Bernadine.

FANNY. Bernadine! I should have known.

STAGEHAND. Don't you think it's anything to do with that! It's because you're brilliant.

STAGEHAND *takes* FANNY*'s hands.*

Enjoy it. It's yours.

FANNY. Thank you, Bernadine.

STAGEHAND. Now, let's get on with the bloody thing!

STAGEHAND *starts redressing.* FANNY *turns to* CLARA.

FANNY. Wait, Clara –

CLARA. I understand. How could anyone be perfect when the world's like this.

FANNY. Do you still think there's space on this stage for two precocious women?

CLARA. At least.

FANNY. Good. Would you do me the honour of sharing the stage with me, Clara?

CLARA. I would.

FANNY. Good! We'll begin with my orchestral work and close with your *remarkable* concerto.

MAESTRO *sticks his head through the curtain..*

MAESTRO. She's seated! The Queen is seated!

MAESTRO*'s head disappears.*

FANNY. Then let's begin! Distribute these to the orchestra please.

STAGEHAND. Oh lovely, they're all nice and mucky. The orchestra'll love that! Come on!

STAGEHAND exits.

FANNY. What are you doing tomorrow, Clara?

CLARA. Nothing.

FANNY. Would you like to come swimming with me?

CLARA. Swimming?

FANNY. Yes. I think I'd like to try swimming. In the *sea!*[39]

WILHELM *runs on – out of breath.*

WILHELM. I made it! Ah, thank goodness! I really wanted to say: I will break your legs!

CLARA. What?

FANNY. Come on, you can watch me from the wings.

CLARA, WILHELM *and* FANNY *exit.*

The Performance

The sound of applause.

FANNY, *dressed as* FELIX, *steps from the audience up onto stage.*

She asks the orchestra (downstage-centre) to stand up and then she turns upstage to face the applause.

She takes a bow, and bows to where the Queen would be.

Then she turns back to the orchestra. She gestures for them to sit down.

FANNY *looks out at each of the individual sections of the orchestra, smiling.*

She takes a breath and brings in the horns.

Music: 'Overture in C-major', Fanny Mendelssohn.[40]

(We should hear as much of this overture as possible.)

As FANNY *conducts she grows – in confidence and stature.*

She seems to fill the theatre.

She reaches up and unfurls her hair.

She tears off her gentleman's jacket.

Her trousers transform into billowing skirts.

In front of the orchestra, the audience and the Queen, she reveals her true self!

It's a magical moment of transformation – the climax of a dream.

She leads the orchestra to the overture's conclusion dressed as FANNY.

It is an image reminiscent of the start of the play.

The lights begin to change, slowly we realise we're back in the Mendelssohn family music room...

The Hensel Family Music Room

FANNY HENSEL *is centre-stage, wielding her baton, conducting an orchestra in her head.*

PAUL *enters upstage and isn't sure whether to interrupt* FANNY.

He can see her conducting but he hears nothing. Eventually...

PAUL. Fanny – ?

The music stops – FANNY*'s arms drop. She stays facing her orchestra throughout the scene.*

I'm sorry to interrupt.

FANNY. What do you need?

PAUL. I'm afraid the inevitable has happened – Sebastian's grown tired of Uncle Paul.[41] He'd like to play with you, I think.

FANNY *smiles*.

FANNY. Send him into the garden to hunt for beetles.[42] I'll be with him shortly.

PAUL. Wilhelm has some students in the garden room.

FANNY. Oh Sebastian won't bother them.

PAUL. Well, I mean to say, it's almost lunch.

FANNY. I see. They won't go hungry, Paul. Was there anything else?

PAUL. Uh... they're saying that people are showing cholera symptoms again.

FANNY. Don't tell Mother.

PAUL. Of course.

FANNY. How is she?

PAUL. Sitting up. Pretending to read.

FANNY (*relieved*). Perhaps some air this afternoon. Will you be here?

PAUL. They need me at the bank.

> PAUL *doesn't leave*.

FANNY. Is something the matter, Paul?

PAUL. No. It's just... Felix has replied – at last.

FANNY. Oh... How is he?

PAUL. I don't know – it's brief.

FANNY. I find myself as afraid of him at forty as I was of Father at fourteen.[43] What does he say?

PAUL. He says that he gives his professional blessing.

> FANNY *takes that in for a moment*.

FANNY. Is that all?

PAUL. He hopes the public only sends you roses and never sand.[44]

FANNY. In his heart he doesn't like it, but at least it's a *word* of encouragement.[45] Leave it on the piano.

> PAUL *does as he's asked*.

PAUL. Your 'Opus 1.[46] How will you choose what should be published first?

FANNY. Lieder I think.

PAUL. Yes, of course, a good idea.

> PAUL *hovers at the door.*

And what's this?

FANNY. An orchestral work.

PAUL. For who?

> FANNY *is silent – the answer is that, in all likelihood, nobody will ever hear it.*
>
> PAUL *reads the silence.*

Do you never feel as though you're pouring water into a sieve?

FANNY *thinks for a moment.*

FANNY. Tell Sebastian that I think I saw a mint beetle yesterday.

PAUL. Right.

FANNY. On the delphinium. I'm just going to hear this phrase, then I'll be out.

PAUL *nods and exits.*

FANNY *takes a moment and re-engages with the orchestra.*

Apologies. Strings – *saltando*, please. It must bounce, yes? Thank you. And can we get a touch more energy in the timpani roll thank you, percussion. Okay, picking up at bar 54. Energy, enthusiasm, passion. And...

FANNY *waves her conductor's baton and brings the orchestra in.*

For the first time, we hear nothing.

We watch FANNY *conduct in silence.*

The lights fade.

Blackout.

End.

Endnotes

1. In the play's opening moments, Fanny is, perhaps, imagining conducting J. S. Bach's work at the Berlin Sing-Akademie. Felix is often credited with 'rescuing' the work of Bach from obscurity. Though perhaps credit could go further up the family genealogy. Fanny and Felix's great-aunt, Sarah Itzig Levy, was an accomplished musician herself and ran an active music salon from her Berlin home which celebrated the work of Bach – she had harpsichord lessons from Bach's eldest son and commissioned work from C.P.E. Bach. Consequently, she joined the Berlin Sing-Akademie (which had been founded to promote German choral work). Is it a coincidence that the director of the Sing-Akademie, Carl Zelter, was hired as Fanny and Felix's music tutor? Their musical education inevitably included lots of Bach's works that had fallen out of fashion – like, for example, this B-minor Mass. It was their grandma, Bella Soloman, who gave Felix a copyist's manuscript of *St Matthew Passion* – so inspired was he, that Felix endeavoured to prepare the monumental work for performance at the Sing-Akademie – a performance that is sometimes seen as the catalyst for the re-evaluation of Bach from 'mathematician' to 'genius'.

2. Zelter, the director of the Sing-Akademie, died in 1832 and Felix was persuaded by his family to apply for the post of director. He didn't particularly want to (he was making a living as a composer and Berlin was seen as being behind the times) but it seemed likely that he'd be a shoe-in – he was talented, studious, had been a member of the akademie since he was a child, he was Zelter's favourite pupil and he'd proven to them that he was a brilliant conductor. Rungenhagan got the job.

3. In a letter to Felix (8 March 1835), Fanny describes Grell, just as Felix does in the play, as '*a blockhead*' or '*a lout*' – depending on the translation. She wasn't a fan of Grell, at various times calling him '*an ugly man*' and writing that he had '*dirty fingers on the piano*'.

4. Queen Victoria did indeed like Mendelssohn's work – he was one of Victoria and Albert's favourite composers and met them personally many times. Knowing that they enjoyed duetting together on the piano he would sometimes arrange his solo work as duets for them to play together.

5. Felix composed the overture to *A Midsummer Night's Dream* during the summer of 1826 and incidental music for the play in 1842. The incidental music included the 'Wedding March' which was made popular when Queen Victoria selected it for the marriage of her daughter to the Prince of Prussia.

6. Music scholar Larry R. Todd suggests that, because Fanny knew she was writing mostly for herself, she was able to plumb the emotions, take risks and create work that is more dissonant than her brother. It's this supposition that prompts Fanny to suggest a more dissonant first chord in bar 6.

ENDNOTES   131

7. Fanny writes in a letter (1 July 1839) that she was worried when Rebecka went for her first swim. Francoise Tillard suggests this might be because great care had been given to the boys' physical education but the two girls' physical education had been overlooked in the Mendelssohn home.

8. In July 1846, Fanny wrote to her brother and said: '*I am no femme libre – still less, alas, part of the <u>Young</u> Germany movement.*' This is probably in reference to the first French feminist journal, of the same name, which had been published in 1832. The first issue appealed to '*Women of the privileged class; you who are young, rich and beautiful.*' In the letter she was asking for her brother's approval to publish her work and my guess is that she felt the need to say something reassuring to him – as she does in the scene.

9. Paul did play the cello privately.

10. Paul listening in (and generally being left out) comes from one of the few stories we have of Paul. Aged four, when the family were returning from a trip to Paris, Paul was left behind at a relay station and rediscovered later on the highway! That said, Paul may have gotten himself left behind; in 1818 a letter from Fanny's cousin described Paul as '*most mischievous*'.

11. Paul received commercial banking training in London and Paris and ended up joining the Mendelssohn family bank in Berlin.

12. The mention of *Othello* here (and all of the Shakespeare mentions in the play) is a reference to a German translation by the literary historian August Wilhelm Schlegel and by the writer Ludwig Tieck, which was published in 1825. It was one of the first translations to be published in German in verse as well as prose and, according to the German Shakespeare historian Hans-Jörg Modlmayr, '*it was made sacrosanct for the educated German bourgeoisie*'. Schlegel was Fanny's Aunt Dorothea's brother-in-law so we can assume there was a copy in the house!

13. Wilhelm Hensel returning from Italy as a Catholic was a genuine worry for Lea. The Mendelssohns were grooming their image as German aristocrats with impeccable morality, which meant sharing the religion of the Prussian government.

14. Fanny didn't share her mother's religious convictions. Before Wilhelm went to Italy he told Fanny about his Catholic temptations who replied that she promised '*to obtain information about the Church*'.

15. This is perhaps the most well-known story of Fanny and Felix. In 1842 Felix was received by Queen Victoria at Buckingham Palace. He writes:

    While they were talking, I looked through the music on the piano and came across my very first volume of lieder. Naturally I asked the Queen to sing me one… she agreed most amiably, and what did she choose? Schoner und schoner [the opening words of 'Italien'].

    He goes on to criticise the Queen's singing, before writing:

    So then I had to admit that Fanny had composed the lied.

16. Lea's line '*it can and must be only an ornament*' is a quote from Fanny's father, Abraham, to a fourteen-year-old Fanny.

17. Theodore Fontane (a German Poet and Novelist) describes Wilhelm:

    He was gay and talkative; anecdotes, toasts, letters in verse form, occasional poetry – all that was at his fingertips. But he was at his best in spontaneous witticisms… He knew better than anyone how to shape poetic inspiration and form epigrammatic puns. He was not a poet but he could have been called 'Wilhelm the rhymer'.

18. In 1822, Lea wrote to Wilhelm and said: '*I did not want to spoil yesterday evening's enjoyment by observing to you that I find it improper for a young man to offer his portrait to a young girl!*' Accepting a portrait was the equivalent of an amorous commitment – and, for Lea, if anyone was to have seen it there might have been scandal.

19. According to Francoise Tillard, on his return from Italy, '*Wilhelm found himself entering a liberal, intellectual milieu that was quite foreign to him*'. And, it would appear that Fanny's circle of friends '*did not look favourably upon this stranger taking over Fanny – Felix least of all*'. She also notes that: '*his puns were not well received*'.

20. Fanny's opening line to Wilhelm, 'You look different', is a reference to Fanny being unlike the traditional nineteenth-century depiction of sweet, gracious young women. As Tillard puts it, '*as the years went by her way of greeting people grew ever more abrupt and less amiable*'. Clara Schumann once described her as '*schroff*', which translates as harsh or abrupt.

21. Tillard suggests that Wilhelm was initially very jealous towards anything dear to Fanny – brothers, intellectual interests and even music. Tillard says he '*didn't understand the household's mentality*' and that, for Fanny, he '*no longer resembled the man she had known*'.

22. Fanny occasionally had bouts of nosebleeds, particularly towards the end of her life. In a letter, dated December 1842, she wrote to Felix she was suffering from '*coughs, sore throats, toothaches, nosebleeds*' – she notes that the nosebleeds '*have weakened me less than last year*' suggesting they were a regular and significant occurrence. Her father, and grandfather, had died of '*cerebral strokes*' (E. R. Gazener and E. A. M. Neugebauer) and good health was, according to Tillard, '*a blessing they [the Mendelssohns] did not possess*'.

23. Lea's response in this scene is reflective of Fanny's father, Abraham, and his attitude after Wilhelm's unsuccessful return from Italy. He wrote to Fanny in late 1828 and said: '*You must school yourself more seriously and eagerly for your true profession, a young woman's only profession; being mistress of the house.*'

24. Tillard poses the question: '*Has anyone heard of Rungenhagen in this day and age?*' It seems that the Sing-Akademie had chosen a risk-free leader. Felix was travelling the world and Rungenhagen had no desire to leave Berlin; Rungenhagen was also older, a Christian and the former director's assistant.

25. '*In polite terms, that they could go hang themselves*' wrote Felix in a letter to Karl Klingeman (his friend and travelling companion) in 1833.

26. Sheila Hayman, Fanny's great-great-great-granddaughter, wrote in the *Guardian* in 2017:

    And, as in a fairytale, this man, ridiculed by the Mendelssohns for his slow wits and inability to hold a tune, turned out to be the hero. He said he wouldn't marry Fanny unless she carried on composing; and every morning of their marriage, before he went off to paint, he would put a piece of blank manuscript paper on her music stand and tell her he wanted to see it filled up when he returned.

27. Felix's response to Fanny in this scene is predominantly drawn from a letter dated 1837 from Felix to his mother on the subject of Fanny publishing her own work. This paragraph, in particular, has lent lots of dialogue:

    …publication is a serious matter (or at least, it ought to be) and I think it should only be done if one intends to present oneself as a composer throughout one's life, and to remain one. This nonetheless implies a succession of works, one following another; if only a few isolated works are published, then only vexation can result – or else it becomes what they call a manuscript for friends, and I don't like that much either. And if I know Fanny, she has neither the wish nor the vocation to become a composer. She is far too self-respecting a woman for that; she sees to her house and thinks not of the public, nor or the musical world – not even of music, except when her primary activity's been carried out.

28. In Peter Sutermeister's biography of Felix, he quotes a letter from Felix to Fanny from around 1830. Fanny, with a young family and without Felix, was struggling for inspiration. Felix's response was:

    You cannot expect a man of my calibre to wish you musical ideas; you are insatiable to complain of their absence; per bacco [good heavens], if you really wanted to, you'd be able to compose…; and, if you don't want to, then why are you complaining so dreadfully? If I had my child to coddle, I wouldn't want to be writing scores…

29. Fanny and Wilhelm had planned to travel to London in the Spring of 1835. They planned to stay with a friend of Felix and Abraham, Mary Alexander – when they wrote to her they asked her not to mention the trip to Abraham. They never made it to England. Abraham's cataracts were getting worse and Fanny and Rebecka had to take turns reading to him and writing his letters, which made a prolonged absence impractical.

30. This meeting of Clara and Fanny is imagined. In 1837, Clara played at the concert hall in Berlin and Fanny writes that she attended the concert – although, Clara had been performing in Berlin since 1832 so it's possible, even likely, that Fanny may have seen her perform earlier. There's no evidence of the two meeting in 1837. They may have met in 1843 when Fanny travelled to Leipzig to visit her brother. Fanny visited the Schumann house and Robert writes in his diary that Fanny's '*mind and depth of feeling speak through her eyes*' – it's fair to assume that Fanny and Clara may have spoken though neither mention the interaction. In 1847 Robert and Clara came to Berlin and, as Berthold Litzman notes, Clara immediately

liked Fanny, writing: '*I have really taken a liking to Frau Hensel and feel particularly drawn to her musically, we are almost always in accord and her conversation is always interesting.*'

31. In the days leading up to his attempted suicide, Robert Schumann experienced auditory hallucinations. Initially hearing repeated notes and other composers' music, eventually voices and visual hallucinations. He was unable to sleep for days. Whilst Clara spoke to doctors he ran from the house in nothing but an overcoat and threw himself into the Rhine. He was rescued by a boat and it was decided that he should be incarcerated in Endenich – he wasn't permitted to see Clara or his family for two years. Brahms, a close friend, read about Robert's attempt on his life and travelled to Clara. He would visit Robert in hospital and look after Clara's children whilst she earned money for the family.

32. It would appear that, in 1847, Felix Mendelssohn (who had been married for ten years) wrote passionate love letters in to the soprano Jenny Lind, '*entreating her to join with him in an adulterous relationship and threatening suicide as a means of exerting pressure upon her*'. This is a quote from the Abstract of Doctor George Biddlecombe's paper entitled 'Secret Letters and a Missing Memorandum: New Light on the Personal Relationship between Felix Mendelssohn and Jenny Lind'.

33. Felix did premiere Clara's orchestral work with the Leipzig Gewandhaus orchestra in 1835. It's incredible – and she was just fifteen when she finished it.

34. Clara's father was a musician and her education under him was very much focused on turning Clara into a star – by all accounts there wasn't much time for anything but music in her life. Though she was always appreciative of him and defended him against criticism, she split from him when she married Robert. Her father wouldn't accept Robert as a son-in-law and so they forced a marriage through the German courts.

35. 'I can't feel my hands.' On Friday 14 May, Fanny was preparing for the rehearsal of that Sunday's concert. Tillard describes what happened next:

    Suddenly her hands refused to obey her. Leaving the piano to another musician, Fanny went into a neighbouring room to soak them in warm vinegar. 'How beautiful it sounds' she said, listening as the rehearsal continued. Thinking she had recovered, she tried to resume rehearsing, not wishing to send for a doctor to treat an illness she thought she knew well. But the paralysis returned, and this time became general. Recognizing her condition, Fanny said only: 'it's a stroke, like Mother had'. She then lost consciousness entirely, never to regain it. She died at 11 o'clock that same evening.

36. London Zoo had opened in 1828 and was becoming a popular attraction, especially after Queen Victoria first visited in 1842.

37. Tillard writes, in reference to Sebasian Hensel's 1879 family history, that: '*Lea's first thought when Fanny was born was to look at the baby's hands, and she declared delightedly that the infant had fingers suitable for playing*

Bach's fuges, Bach'sche Fugenfinger.'

38. There's no evidence to suggest Queen Victoria liked a sarcastic parrot at London Zoo. We do know that she paid many visits to the zoo and was fascinated and repulsed by an orangutan called Jenny who she described as a: *'frightful and painfully disagreeable human'*.

39. In 1839, Fanny and Rebecka went to Heringsdorf and swam in the sea for the first time. According to Yvonne Knibiehler, *'the vogue for bathing in the sea was probably what accelerated the emancipation of the female body'*. Fanny appears to have enjoyed the experience she and Rebecka grew closer after sharing this liberating experience.

40. Fanny's 'Overture in C-major' was probably written between 1830–1832 (certainly no later, as in 1834 she says *'It was great fun to hear the piece for the first time in 2 years'*). In a letter, dated 1834, she writes about conducting it:

    Mother has certainly told you about the Konigstadt Orchestra on Saturday and how I stood up there with a baton in my hand like a Jupiter tonans. That came about in the following way. Lecerf had his scholars play and smashed his finger to pieces in the process, then I went out and brought your little white baton and handed it to him. Later my overture was played and I sat at the piano, then the devil in the form of Leceref whispered to me to take the little baton in my hand. Had I not been so horribly shy, and embarrassed with every stroke I would have been able to conduct reasonably well… people seemed to like it – they were very kind, praised me, criticised a few impractical passages and will return again next Saturday.

41. Uncle Paul looking after Sebastian is a reference to the role Paul took on in the family after the other siblings' deaths. When Felix died, Paul took Felix's sons to live with him. And when both Rebecka and her husband died, Paul took charge of Rebecka's daughter Flora.

42. 'Tell Sebastian to hunt for beetles' is a reference to the young child's favourite pastime of collecting insects.

43. Fanny wrote to Felix in 1846: *'At the age of forty I'm as afraid of my brothers as I was of Father when I was fourteen'*.

44. It took Felix more than a month to reply to Fanny when she wrote and told him that she was going to begin publishing work under her own name. When he did reply the letter was short and unenthusiastic. He wrote: *'[I] give you my professional blessing'* and *'may the public only send you roses and never sand'*.

45. Fanny wrote in her diary: *'Felix has finally written to me and conferred his professional blessing in a very friendly way; I know that in his heart he doesn't like it, but I'm delighted that he's finally offered me a word of encouragement'*.

46. Fanny's 'Opus 1' was titled 'Sechs Lieder' ['Six Lieder'].

A Nick Hern Book

Fanny first published in Great Britain as a paperback original in 2024 by Nick Hern Books Limited, The Glasshouse, 49a Goldhawk Road, London W12 8QP, in association with the Watermill Theatre and RJG Productions

Fanny copyright © 2024 Calum Finlay

Calum Finlay has asserted his right to be identified as the author of this work

Cover artwork by Rebecca Pitt. Photography by Michael Wharley

Designed and typeset by Nick Hern Books, London
Printed in Great Britain by Mimeo Ltd, Huntingdon, Cambridgeshire PE29 6XX

A CIP catalogue record for this book is available from the British Library

ISBN 978 1 83904 362 8

CAUTION All rights whatsoever in this play are strictly reserved. Requests to reproduce the text in whole or in part should be addressed to the publisher.

Amateur Performing Rights Applications for performance, including readings and excerpts, by amateurs in the English language should be addressed to the Performing Rights Manager, Nick Hern Books, The Glasshouse, 49a Goldhawk Road, London W12 8QP, *tel* +44 (0)20 8749 4953, *email* rights@nickhernbooks.co.uk, except as follows:

Australia: ORiGiN Theatrical, *tel* +61 (2) 8514 5201, *email* enquiries@originmusic.com.au, *web* www.origintheatrical.com.au

New Zealand: Play Bureau, 20 Rua Street, Mangapapa, Gisborne 4010, *tel* +64 21 258 3998, *email* info@playbureau.com

Professional Performing Rights Rights Applications for performance by professionals in any medium and in any language throughout the world should be addressed in the first instance to Nick Hern Books, see contact details above.

No performance of any kind may be given unless a licence has been obtained. Applications should be made before rehearsals begin. Publication of this play does not necessarily indicate its availability for amateur performance.

www.nickhernbooks.co.uk/environmental-policy

www.nickhernbooks.co.uk

facebook.com/nickhernbooks

twitter.com/nickhernbooks